Oracle Debugging
A Comprehensive Guide to Debugging Solutions

Oracle In-Focus Series

Ben Prusinski

RAMPANT
TECHPRESS

I would like to dedicate this book to my parents and Scot Conrad who mentored me on many aspects of the Oracle database. I also want to extend my appreciation to all friends and Oracle professionals who spend their days working in the trenches to support mission critical databases.

Ben Prusinski

Oracle Debugging
A Comprehensive Guide to Debugging Solutions

By Ben Prusinski

Oracle In-Focus Series: Book 34

Series Editor: Donald K. Burleson

Production Manager: Robin Rademacher

Production Editor: Valerre Aquitaine

Cover Design: Janet Burleson

Printing History: May 2011 for First Edition

Oracle, Oracle7, Oracle8, Oracle8i, Oracle9i, Oracle10g and Oracle 11g are trademarks of Oracle Corporation.

Many of the designations used by computer vendors to distinguish their products are claimed as Trademarks. All names known by Rampant TechPress to be trademark names appear in this text as initial caps.

The information provided by the authors of this work is believed to be accurate and reliable. However, because of the possibility of human error by our authors and staff, Rampant TechPress cannot guarantee the accuracy or completeness of any information included in this work and is not responsible for any errors, omissions, or inaccurate results obtained from the use of information or scripts in this work.

ISBN 10: 0-9823061-4-8
ISBN 13: 978-0-9823061-4-7
Library of Congress Control Number: 2009930094

Table of Contents

Using the Online Code Depot

Purchase of this book provides complete access to the online code depot that contains sample code scripts. Any code depot scripts in this book are located at the following URL in zip format and ready to load and use:

rampant.cc/debug.htm

If technical assistance is needed with downloading or accessing the scripts, please contact Rampant TechPress at rtp@rampant.cc.

Conventions Used in this Book

It is critical for any technical publication to follow rigorous standards and employ consistent punctuation conventions to make the text easy to read. However, this is not an easy task. Within database terminology, there are many types of notations that can confuse a reader. For example, some Oracle utilities such as STATSPACK and TKPROF are always spelled in CAPITAL letters, while Oracle parameters and procedures have varying naming conventions in the database documentation. It is also important to remember that many database commands are case sensitive, and are always left in their original executable form, and never altered with italics or capitalization.

Hence, all Rampant TechPress books follow these conventions:

Parameters – All database parameters will be lowercase italics. Exceptions to this rule are parameter arguments that are commonly capitalized (KEEP pool, TKPROF), these will be left in ALL CAPS.

Variables – All procedural language (e.g. PL/SQL) program variables and arguments will also remain in lowercase italics (dbms_job, dbms_utility).

Tables & dictionary objects – All data dictionary objects are referenced in lowercase italics (dba_indexes, v$sql). This includes all v$ and x$ views (x$kcbcbh, v$parameter) and dictionary views (dba_tables, user_indexes).

SQL – All SQL is formatted for easy use in the code depot, and all SQL is displayed in lowercase. The main SQL terms (select, from, where, group by, order by, having) will always appear on a separate line.

Programs & Products – All products and programs that are known to the author are capitalized according to the vendor specifications (CentOS, VMware, Oracle, etc). All names known by Rampant TechPress to be trademark names appear in this text as initial caps. References to UNIX are always made in uppercase.

Acknowledgements

This type of highly technical reference book requires the dedicated efforts of many people. Even though we are the authors, our work ends when we deliver the content. After each chapter is delivered, several Oracle DBAs carefully review and correct the technical content. After the technical review, experienced copy editors polish the grammar and syntax.

The finished work is then reviewed as page proofs and turned over to the production manager, who arranges the creation of the online code depot and manages the cover art, printing distribution, and warehousing.

In short, the authors play a small role in the development of this book, and I need to thank and acknowledge everyone who helped bring this book to fruition:

Robin Rademacher for production management including the coordination of the cover art, page proofing, printing, and distribution.

Valerre Q Aquitaine for help in the production of the page proofs.

Janet Burleson for exceptional cover design and graphics.

John Lavender for assistance with the web site and for creating the code depot and the online shopping cart for this book.

With my sincerest thanks,

Ben Prusinski

Introduction to Oracle 11g Debugging

Oracle databases are by nature extremely complex beasts. The fact that the Oracle database interacts with both third party applications as well as the host operating system and network systems makes the level of complexity even greater. With each new database release, Oracle introduces many new features, adding even further to the chain of complexity. It is nearly impossible for even the most experienced Oracle DBA to master all facets of the Oracle environment without consulting the Oracle documentation via Metalink or the Oracle documentation online.

A Comprehensive Guide to Debugging

As such, this book is the result of more than a decade of real world Oracle DBA experience from the trenches and will serve to fill in the gaps left behind by the Oracle documentation. It will present a comprehensive guide to debugging and problem resolution for difficult Oracle issues. While no single guide is able to cover every detail for Oracle, this will present a best practices approach to solving common and unusual Oracle issues.

The new Oracle 11g Release 1 came out in July 2007 for public general release on Linux and Windows platforms. The focus of this book will be on how to best leverage poorly documented as well as undocumented and hidden utilities, tools and features with Oracle 11g that previously either had scant documentation or have been exclusively in the realm of Oracle internal support engineers. Also to be touched upon are some of the most useful new features within Oracle 11g as they pertain to the discussion for debugging Oracle 11g. Finally, while previous releases will not be the primary focus of this book, the majority of the tools and tips offered will be available and useful for all major Oracle releases previous to 11g.

New Features for Debugging Oracle 11g

Oracle 11g has implemented many new tuning and debugging features over previous database releases. The top new feature for debugging tough Oracle 11g problems exists with the new Automatic Diagnostic Repository (ADR) tool for monitoring and viewing Oracle trace and diagnostic files.

This new tool, which is available via both command line and from within Enterprise Manager Grid Control, provides comprehensive reporting and monitoring functions for Oracle trace files, alert log reporting and other features for the Oracle 11g database environment. Prior to Oracle 11g, trace files were stored by default under the *user_dump_dest* directory. Also before Oracle 11g, the *alert.log* text based file which contains details on the status of the Oracle database were stored by default under the background dump destination directory and now is referenced by a single initialization parameter called *diagnostic_dest*. The previous release parameters for *background_dump_dest*, *core_dump_dest*, and *user_dump_dest* have been deprecated and replaced by the single parameter *diagnostic_dest*. Now with Oracle 11g, these files are managed under the ADR directory structure and can be viewed by the ADR tool. The base monitoring file is stored in XML format in a file called *log.xml*. By default, the diagnostic directory structure is tied to the *oracle home*, *oracle base* and *oracle_sid* environment variables.

```
SQL> show parameter diagnostic_dest

NAME                                 TYPE        VALUE
------------------------------------ ----------- --------------------
diagnostic_dest                      string      /u01/app/oracle
```

The Oracle 11g ADR uses a home directory to centralize log file maintenance operations. By default, the ADR home directory is located under the directory structure:

```
<ADR_BASE>/diag/rdbms/<db_name>/<instance_id>.
```

To show the home directory details for ADR, log on to the command
line tool ADRCI as follows:

```
[oracle@raclinux1 ~]$ adrci

ADRCI: Release 11.1.0.6.0 - Beta on Tue Jul 29 00:07:57 2008

Copyright (c) 1982, 2007, Oracle.  All rights reserved.

ADR base = "/u01/app/oracle"
adrci> show home

ADR Homes:
diag/rdbms/ora11g/ora11g
diag/rdbms/ora11g/ORA11G
diag/rdbms/default/ORA11G
diag/rdbms/unknown/ORA11G
diag/rdbms/stdby1/stdby1
diag/clients/user_oracle/host_3681296775_11
diag/clients/user_unknown/host_411310321_11
diag/tnslsnr/raclinux1/listener
diag/tnslsnr/raclinux1/listener1
diag/tnslsnr/raclinux1/listener_stdby1
```

In addition to using the ADRCI *show home* command, the location for
the ADR configuration can be displayed using the *v$diag_info* view as
shown in the below example.

```
Oracle Database 11g Enterprise Edition Release 11.1.0.6.0 - Production
With the Partitioning, OLAP, Data Mining and Real Application Testing
options

SQL> col name format a20
SQL> col value format a50 word_wrapped
SQL> select name, value
  2  from
  3  v$diag_info;

NAME                 VALUE
-------------------- -------------------------------------------------
Diag Enabled         TRUE
ADR Base             /u01/app/oracle
ADR Home             /u01/app/oracle/diag/rdbms/ora11g/ORA11G
Diag Trace           /u01/app/oracle/diag/rdbms/ora11g/ORA11G/trace
Diag Alert           /u01/app/oracle/diag/rdbms/ora11g/ORA11G/alert
Diag Incident        /u01/app/oracle/diag/rdbms/ora11g/ORA11G/incident
Diag Cdump           /u01/app/oracle/diag/rdbms/ora11g/ORA11G/cdump
Health Monitor       /u01/app/oracle/diag/rdbms/ora11g/ORA11G/hm
Default Trace File   /u01/app/oracle/diag/rdbms/ora11g/ORA11G/trace/ORA
                     11G_ora_28603.trc
```

The above query against the *v$diag_info* view provides the DBA with the default locations for the diagnostic trace, alert, incident, core dump, ADR home, ADR base, and health monitor files for Oracle 11g.

If the *log.xml* file is examined, it should be noticed that the default *xml alert.log* file contains all of the entries that are also contained in the text based *alert.log* file which is available for backward compatibility with previous releases.

```
SQL> !ls /u01/app/oracle/diag/rdbms/ora11g/ORA11G/alert
log.xml

SQL> !view /u01/app/oracle/diag/rdbms/ora11g/ORA11G/alert/log.xml
<msg time='2008-06-09T18:34:25.057-04:00' org_id='oracle' comp_id='rdbms'
 msg_id='opistr_real:871:3971575317' type='NOTIFICATION' group='startup'
 level='16' pid='7457' version='1'>
 <txt>Starting ORACLE instance (normal)
 </txt>
</msg>
<msg time='2008-06-09T18:34:25.840-04:00' org_id='oracle' comp_id='rdbms'
 msg_id='ksunfy:13399:2937430291' type='NOTIFICATION' group='startup'
 level='16' pid='7457'>
 <txt>LICENSE_MAX_SESSION = 0
 </txt>
</msg>
<msg time='2008-06-09T18:34:25.840-04:00' org_id='oracle' comp_id='rdbms'
 msg_id='ksunfy:13400:4207019197' type='NOTIFICATION' group='startup'
 level='16' pid='7457'>
 <txt>LICENSE_SESSIONS_WARNING = 0
 </txt>
</msg>
<msg time='2008-06-09T18:34:25.918-04:00' org_id='oracle' comp_id='rdbms'
 msg_id='kcsnfy:323:968333812' type='NOTIFICATION' group='startup'
 level='16' pid='7457'>
 <txt>Picked latch-free SCN scheme 2
 </txt>
</msg>
<msg time='2008-06-09T18:34:26.494-04:00' org_id='oracle' comp_id='rdbms'
 msg id='kcrrdini:15230:1211400554' type='NOTIFICATION' group='startup'
 level='16' pid='7457'>
```

Since the format of the *log.xml* file is not intended for viewing in xml format, it is advised to use the ADRCI interface to view log files. Returning to the ADR interface via the ADRCI command tool, the help contents can be dumped to provide a list of commands available with ADR as shown in the below figure. Also, use the *help extended* command to display more details.

```
[oracle@raclinux1 ~]$ adrci
```

```
ADRCI: Release 11.1.0.6.0 - Beta on Tue Jul 29 00:29:52 2008

Copyright (c) 1982, 2007, Oracle.  All rights reserved.

ADR base = "/u01/app/oracle"
adrci> help extended

 HELP [topic]

    Available Topics:
          BEGIN BACKUP
          CD
          DDE
          DEFINE
          DESCRIBE
          END BACKUP
          LIST DEFINE
          MERGE ALERT
          MERGE FILE
          QUERY
          SET COLUMN
          SHOW CATALOG
          SHOW DUMP
          SHOW SECTION
          SHOW TRACE
          SHOW TRACEMAP
          SWEEP
          UNDEFINE
          VIEW

adrci> help

HELP [topic]

    Available Topics:
          CREATE REPORT
          ECHO
          EXIT
          HELP
          HOST
          IPS
          PURGE
          RUN
          SET BASE
          SET BROWSER
          SET CONTROL
          SET ECHO
          SET EDITOR
          SET HOMES | HOME | HOMEPATH
          SET TERMOUT
          SHOW ALERT
          SHOW BASE
          SHOW CONTROL
          SHOW HM_RUN
          SHOW HOMES | HOME | HOMEPATH
          SHOW INCDIR
          SHOW INCIDENT
          SHOW PROBLEM
```

```
SHOW REPORT
SHOW TRACEFILE
SPOOL
```

There are other commands intended to be used directly by Oracle. Type *help extended* to see the list:

```
adrci>
```

If one wants to find specific help on a particular topic with ADR, issue the command *help* followed by the topic as shown in the next example.

```
adrci> help dde create incident

  Usage:  DDE CREATE INCIDENT TYPE <type>

  Purpose: Create an incident of specified type.
          If the incident type is associated with an action, the action
will be automatically recommended for the new incident.

  Arguments:
    <type>:  Incident type

  Notes:
    The relation DDE_USER_INCIDENT_TYPE shows available incident types.

  Example:
    dde create incident type wrong_results
```

ADR is basically the alert monitoring on steroids. It further allows for the packaging of incidents and reports to be sent to Oracle customer support for analysis and problem resolution. To view the alert log reports in ADR, issue the *show alert* command:

```
adrci> show alert

Choose the alert log from the following homes to view:

1: diag/rdbms/ora11g/ora11g
2: diag/rdbms/ora11g/ORA11G
3: diag/rdbms/default/ORA11G
4: diag/rdbms/unknown/ORA11G
5: diag/rdbms/stdby1/stdby1
6: diag/clients/user_oracle/host_3681296775_11
7: diag/clients/user_unknown/host_411310321_11
8: diag/tnslsnr/raclinux1/listener
9: diag/tnslsnr/raclinux1/listener1
10: diag/tnslsnr/raclinux1/listener_stdby1
Q: to quit
```

Please select option 1:

```
Output the results to file: /tmp/alert_30297_3086_ora11g_1.ado

2008-05-18 18:54:11.768000 -04:00
Starting ORACLE instance (normal)
2008-05-18 18:54:12.946000 -04:00
LICENSE_MAX_SESSION = 0
LICENSE_SESSIONS_WARNING = 0
Shared memory segment for instance monitoring created
Picked latch-free SCN scheme 2
2008-05-18 18:54:14.823000 -04:00
Using LOG_ARCHIVE_DEST_1 parameter default value as
"/tmp/alert_30297_3086_ora11g_1.ado" 1274L, 53223C
```

The ADR monitoring system can also be understood in terms of examination of the following *v$* views:

- *v$hm_check*

- *v$hm_check_param*

- *v$hm_finding*

- *v$hm_info*

- *v$hm_recommendation*

- *v$hm_run*

Now that the basic monitoring functions available with the ADR tools for Oracle 11g have been shown, next to be reviewed is how ADR manages incidents with Oracle 11g. Incidents refer to critical database errors that usually generate core dump files. In particular, ADR will automatically generate an incident report for most internal error conditions such as those for ORA-00600, ORA-00700, and ORA-07445. When such internal errors occur, an incident package can be assembled with ADR to send to Oracle internal support for analysis and resolution. The ability to create and package incidents is a robust feature provided by ADR that quickly assists the busy DBA in sending diagnostic files to Oracle support during crisis situations.

The following example will illustrate how to use the incident feature with ADR for sending critical diagnostic information to Oracle Support.

The first step is to set the ADR home directory since the *ips create package* command supports only a single ADR home at one time.

```
adrci> set homepath diag/rdbms/ora11g/ora11g
adrci> show homes

ADR Homes:
diag/rdbms/ora11g/ora11g

adrci> show incident

ADR Home = /u01/app/oracle/diag/rdbms/ora11g/ora11g:
*************************************************************************
0 rows fetched

adrci> ips create package

Created package 1 without any contents, correlation level typical
```

Once the new incident package is created as in the previous example, it is now time to add outstanding incidents to the package.

The following ADR commands are used to add the incident and create the necessary zip files to send to Oracle support for analysis.

```
ips add incident <incident_id> package <package_id>
ips generate package <package_id> in <directory>
```

The ADR configuration settings for the incident package creation can be viewed with the *ips show* command:

```
adrci> ips show configuration

************************************************************
IPS CONFIGURATION PARAMETER
************************************************************
-----------------------------------------------------------
PARAMETER INFORMATION:
    PARAMETER_ID            1
    NAME                    CUTOFF_TIME
    DESCRIPTION             Maximum age for an incident to be
considered for inclusion
    UNIT                    Days
    VALUE                   90
    DEFAULT_VALUE           90


-----------------------------------------------------------
************************************************************
IPS CONFIGURATION PARAMETER
************************************************************
```

```
------------------------------------------------------------
PARAMETER INFORMATION:
    PARAMETER_ID                2
    NAME                        NUM_EARLY_INCIDENTS
    DESCRIPTION                 How many incidents to get in the early
part of the range
    UNIT                        Number
    VALUE                       3
    DEFAULT_VALUE               3


------------------------------------------------------------
************************************************************
IPS CONFIGURATION PARAMETER
************************************************************
------------------------------------------------------------
PARAMETER INFORMATION:
    PARAMETER_ID                3
    NAME                        NUM_LATE_INCIDENTS
    DESCRIPTION                 How many incidents to get in the late part
of the range
    UNIT                        Number
    VALUE                       3
    DEFAULT_VALUE               3


------------------------------------------------------------
************************************************************
IPS CONFIGURATION PARAMETER
************************************************************
------------------------------------------------------------
PARAMETER INFORMATION:
    PARAMETER_ID                4
    NAME                        INCIDENT_TIME_WINDOW
    DESCRIPTION                 Incidents this close to each other are
considered correlated
    UNIT                        Minutes
    VALUE                       5
    DEFAULT_VALUE               5


------------------------------------------------------------
************************************************************
IPS CONFIGURATION PARAMETER
************************************************************
------------------------------------------------------------
PARAMETER INFORMATION:
    PARAMETER_ID                5
    NAME                        PACKAGE_TIME_WINDOW
    DESCRIPTION                 Time window for content inclusion is from
x hours before first included incident to x hours after last incident
    UNIT                        Hours
    VALUE                       24
    DEFAULT_VALUE               24


------------------------------------------------------------
************************************************************
IPS CONFIGURATION PARAMETER
************************************************************
------------------------------------------------------------
PARAMETER INFORMATION:
```

```
    PARAMETER_ID                    6
    NAME                            DEFAULT_CORRELATION_LEVEL
    DESCRIPTION                     Default correlation level for packages
    UNIT                            Number
    VALUE                           2
    DEFAULT_VALUE                   2

--------------------------------------------------------
********************************************************
IPS CONFIGURATION PARAMETER
********************************************************
--------------------------------------------------------
PARAMETER INFORMATION:
    PARAMETER_ID                    7
    NAME                            PURGE_ENABLED
    DESCRIPTION                     If automatic purging is allowed for the
IPS schema
    UNIT                            Number
    VALUE                           1
    DEFAULT_VALUE                   1

--------------------------------------------------------
adrci>
```

The zipped files can then be uploaded to Metalink for coordination with Oracle customer support.

In addition to the ADR command line, Enterprise Manager provides a facility called the EM Support Workbench that can be used for managing incidents and reports to send to Oracle internal customer support.

Due to the vast array of commands and functions available with the powerful new ADR monitoring tools, it is recommended that the Oracle 11g documentation be consulted for the comprehensive syntax and list of functions available for more details on this robust new tool for Oracle 11g monitoring.

 User ID = book, Password = reader

Undocumented Tools

Among the many undocumented tools within the Oracle 11g release that will be covered is the BBED utility for analysis and problem resolution events with Oracle. One note of caution: when using undocumented tools such as BBED, it is critical that extreme care be exercised or database corruption and/or data loss can result. The prudent usage of these utilities should be taken in a non-production environment for testing as well as used with guidance from Oracle customer support.

Poorly Documented Tools

Oracle provides many excellent tools for analysis, monitoring and performance tuning. However, many of these utilities are poorly documented or unknown by most Oracle DBAs. Internal database issues and problems such as the infamous ORA-0600 errors can be investigated and diagnosed with tools such as Oradebug.

Among the poorly documented tools that will be covered are Oradebug, TKPROF, Autotrace, and the *dbms_sqltune* packages for Oracle 11g. In addition, how to utilize the *dbms_stats* package within the context of Oracle 11g to best tune the database environments will be examined.

Summary

In this chapter, the following topics have been introduced concerning the new features for debugging and troubleshooting Oracle 11g:

- Automatic Diagnostic Monitor (ADR) tool for Oracle 11g

- Overview of undocumented and hidden features for Oracle

The following chapters will illustrate the nuts and bolts of how to debug complex Oracle database problems using these undocumented and hidden Oracle features.

Performance Tuning Tools for Oracle 11g

In the last chapter, the Automatic Diagnostic Repository (ADR) monitoring utility new to Oracle 11g for viewing Oracle trace, alert and output files was detailed. In this chapter, how to best leverage additional tools available in Oracle database environments to solve difficult tuning issues will be covered. In particular, the focus will be on the usage of AutoTrace, SQL Trace, TKPROF, *dbms_stats* and SQL tuning packages with Oracle 11g. As a side benefit most, if not all, of these tools are available with earlier releases for Oracle databases such as 9i and 10g. However, syntax and options may differ between releases since the 11g version of Oracle.

AutoTrace

Oracle provides many useful performance-monitoring tools to tune complex database environments. AutoTrace is what can be called a quick and dirty tool that can provide a fast assessment for statistics and execution plans for SQL and PL/SQL queries. Unlike SQL trace, TKPROF, and other more complex tuning tools, AutoTrace is simpler and easier to use. No trace events need to be configured and no dump files need to be generated to obtain the important performance results for query statistics or execution plans. To use the AutoTrace utility within Oracle, open a new SQL*Plus session and use the *set autotrace on* command:

```
[oracle@raclinux1 ~]$ sqlplus "/as sysdba"

SQL*Plus: Release 11.1.0.6.0 - Production on Tue Aug 12 01:19:38 2008

Copyright (c) 1982, 2007, Oracle.  All rights reserved.
Connected to:
Oracle Database 11g Enterprise Edition Release 11.1.0.6.0 - Production
With the Partitioning, OLAP, Data Mining and Real Application Testing
options
```

```
SQL> set autotrace

Usage: SET AUTOT[RACE] {OFF | ON | TRACE[ONLY]} [EXP[LAIN]] [STAT[ISTICS]]
```

Options for AutoTrace allow one to do an explain on the query, collect performance statistics or do a trace on the query only to display the execution plan without actually running the query. Below is an example of how to use AutoTrace to show the statistics and execution plan for the following figure query.

```
SQL> set autotrace on
SQL> select * from scott.dept;

    DEPTNO DNAME          LOC
---------- -------------- -------------
        10 ACCOUNTING     NEW YORK
        20 RESEARCH       DALLAS
        30 SALES          CHICAGO
        40 OPERATIONS     BOSTON

Execution Plan
------------------------------------------------------------
Plan hash value: 3383998547
------------------------------------------------------------
| Id | Operation         | Name | Rows | Bytes | Cost (%CPU)| Time     |
------------------------------------------------------------
|  0 | SELECT STATEMENT  |      |    4 |    80 |    3   (0)| 00:00:01 |
|  1 | TABLE ACCESS FULL | DEPT |    4 |    80 |    3   (0)| 00:00:01 |
------------------------------------------------------------
Statistics
------------------------------------------------------------
          0  recursive calls
          0  db block gets
          8  consistent gets
          0  physical reads
          0  redo size
        654  bytes sent via SQL*Net to client
        420  bytes received via SQL*Net from client
          2  SQL*Net roundtrips to/from client
          0  sorts (memory)
          0  sorts (disk)
          4  rows processed

SQL> set autotrace off
```

AutoTrace can be toggled off and on by using the *set autotrace off* and *set autotrace on* commands within the SQL*Plus session. It is an excellent tool for busy DBAs since it combines many of the tuning functions of the explain plan with tkprof in one tool. As much data can be collected as needed or simply obtain the execution plan as shown in the following example.

```
SQL> set autotrace on explain
SQL> select * from scott.salgrade;

     GRADE      LOSAL       HISAL
---------- ---------- ----------
         1        700        1200
         2       1201        1400
         3       1401        2000
         4       2001        3000
         5       3001        9999


Execution Plan
----------------------------------------------------------
Plan hash value: 2489195056
----------------------------------------------------------
| Id | Operation         | Name     | Rows | Bytes | Cost (%CPU)| Time     |
----------------------------------------------------------
|  0 | SELECT STATEMENT  |          |    5 |    50 |    3   (0)| 00:00:01 |
|  1 |  TABLE ACCESS FULL| SALGRADE |    5 |    50 |    3   (0)| 00:00:01 |
----------------------------------------------------------

SQL> set autotrace off
```

In the previous example, the goal was to obtain the execution plan for the query as well as details on the associated costs from the Oracle 11g Cost Based Optimizer (CBO) and not comprehensive performance statistics.

SQL Trace

Oracle 11g provides a trace facility for tracing SQL queries using different Oracle events for specific tracing activities.

Note: The SQL trace tool is also available with earlier releases of Oracle. However, syntax may differ slightly. SQL trace can be executed from either the session level within SQL*Plus or for the Oracle 11g instance level.

To set a SQL trace at the instance level, use the *alter system* commands within SQL*Plus and for session level tracing, set the trace using *alter session* commands. Due to the performance impact on Oracle when using an instance level trace, it is recommended to run SQL trace at the session layer to minimize load on the Oracle database system. For example, if SQL queries are to be traced via an SQL trace, the event 10046 would be invoked from the trace to examine SQL query performance. To examine the Oracle Cost Based Optimizer (CBO) behavior on queries, trace event 10053.

Next is an example illustrating how to trace SQL statements via the Oracle 11g SQL trace feature. First, open a new SQL*Plus session with Oracle 11g and set up a few key Oracle 11g tuning parameters for the SQL trace.

```
SQL> show parameter user_dump_dest

NAME                            TYPE        VALUE
user_dump_dest                  string      /u01/app/oracle/diag/rdbms/ora
                                            11g/ORA11G/trace
SQL> alter session set tracefile_identifier='10046_trace';

Session altered.

SQL> alter session set timed_statistics=true;

Session altered.

SQL> alter session set statistics_level=all;

Session altered.

SQL> alter session set max_dump_file_size=unlimited;

Session altered.

SQL> alter session set events '10046 trace name context forever, level 12';

Session altered.
```

Bear in mind that the default location for the SQL trace *raw dump* files will be the *user_dump_dest* directory for Oracle 11g. Once the trace is enabled as shown above, Oracle will dump output to a raw *text trace* file. While the raw trace file is readable, it is advised to format the trace file using the TKPROF utility which will be used after implementing SQL trace. Oracle 11g allows for multiple statistics collection levels specified by the *statistics_level* parameter. If the DBA wants to see all data dumped by SQL trace, the setting for this parameter is to the ALL value. It can also be set to TYPICAL or BASIC for less dump information collected by the SQL trace activity.

Additionally, since trace dump files can grow large, it is also recommended to set the Oracle 11g parameter *max_dump_file_size* to unlimited so no errors occur with the trace activity. Be advised that adequate file systems and disk space will need to be available for the dump file or errors will occur during the tracing should the dump file grow larger than the available space. These trace files can grow quite large - up to several megabytes or greater in size depending on the duration and amount of trace activity generated in the dump file. Next to be generated are some SQL trace activity in an example with a review of the output trace file for a SQL trace session.

```
select * from oe.products;

------------------------------------------------------------------------
SUPPLIER_ID PRODUCT_STATUS        LIST_PRICE MIN_PRICE
----------- -------------------- ---------- ----------
CATALOG_URL
------------------------------------------------------

288 rows selected.

select * from oe.orders;

      2457
01-NOV-99 01.22.16.162632 AM
direct          118           5      21586.2          159

105 rows selected.
```

Now end the trace session and review the trace file generated by the SQL trace session.

```
SQL> alter session set events '10046 trace name context off';

Session altered.

SQL> exit

Disconnected from Oracle Database 11g Enterprise Edition Release 11.1.0.6.0
- Production
With the Partitioning, OLAP, Data Mining and Real Application Testing
options
[oracle@raclinux1 ~]$
```

Note here that one can either exit from SQL*Plus or use the *trace name context off* command with the particular trace event, i.e. 10046, if remaining connected to Oracle via SQL*Plus.

The SQL trace generates a raw trace file under the *user_dump_dest* directory specified by this Oracle *initialization* parameter. The SQL trace file can be viewed and opened with a favorite OS text editor such as vi or emacs in UNIX/Linux or with notepad in Windows. The sample SQL trace file is shown next.

```
[oracle@raclinux1 ~]$ cd /u01/app/oracle/diag/rdbms/ora11g/ORA11G/trace

[oracle@raclinux1 trace]$ ls -altr *10046*
-rw-r-----  1 oracle oinstall     754 Aug 13 00:27
ORA11G_ora_3945_10046_trace.trm
-rw-r-----  1 oracle oinstall  128014 Aug 13 00:27
ORA11G_ora_3945_10046_trace.trc
[oracle@raclinux1 trace]$
[oracle@raclinux1 trace]$ view ORA11G_ora_3945_10046_trace.trc
Trace file
/u01/app/oracle/diag/rdbms/ora11g/ORA11G/trace/ORA11G_ora_3945_10046_trace.t
rc
Oracle Database 11g Enterprise Edition Release 11.1.0.6.0 - Production
With the Partitioning, OLAP, Data Mining and Real Application Testing
options
ORACLE_HOME = /u01/app/oracle/product/11.1.0/11g
System name:    Linux
Node name:      raclinux1.us.oracle.com
Release:        2.6.9-5.EL
Version:        #1 Sun Jun 12 12:31:23 IDT 2005
Machine:        i686
Instance name: ORA11G
Redo thread mounted by this instance: 1
Oracle process number: 18
Unix process pid: 3945, image: oracle@raclinux1.us.oracle.com (TNS V1-V3)


*** 2008-08-13 00:07:18.323
*** SESSION ID:(155.3) 2008-08-13 00:07:18.323
*** CLIENT ID:() 2008-08-13 00:07:18.323
*** SERVICE NAME:(SYS$USERS) 2008-08-13 00:07:18.323
*** MODULE NAME:(Oracle Enterprise Manager.pin EM plsql) 2008-08-13
00:07:18.323
*** ACTION NAME:(start) 2008-08-13 00:07:18.323

WAIT #31: nam='SQL*Net message to client' ela= 10 driver id=1650815232
#bytes=1 p3=0 obj#=70310 tim=1218600448747669

*** 2008-08-13 00:19:21.196
WAIT #31: nam='SQL*Net message from client' ela= 722873162 driver
id=1650815232 #bytes=1 p3=0 obj#=70310 tim=1218601171621453
=====================
PARSING IN CURSOR #20 len=198 dep=2 uid=0 oct=3 lid=0 tim=1218601171636887
hv=4125641360 ad='376419d4' sqlid='04xtrk7uyhknh'
select obj#,type#,ctime,mtime,stime,status,dataobj#,flags,oid$, spare1,
spare2 from obj$ where owner#=:1 and name=:2 and namespace=:3 and
remoteowner is null and linkname is null and subname is null
END OF STMT
PARSE #20:c=0,e=1890,p=0,cr=0,cu=0,mis=1,r=0,dep=2,og=4,tim=1218601171636875
BINDS #20:
 Bind#0
  oacdty=02 mxl=22(22) mxlc=00 mal=00 scl=00 pre=00
  oacflg=08 fl2=0001 frm=00 csi=00 siz=24 off=0
  kxsbbbfp=b6c9eaa0  bln=22  avl=01  flg=05
```

```
    value=0
  Bind#1
   oacdty=01 mxl=32(05) mxlc=00 mal=00 scl=00 pre=00
   oacflg=18 fl2=0001 frm=01 csi=178 siz=32 off=0
   kxsbbbfp=b6c9ea74  bln=32  avl=05  flg=05
   value="VIEW$"
  Bind#2
   oacdty=02 mxl=22(22) mxlc=00 mal=00 scl=00 pre=00
   oacflg=08 fl2=0001 frm=00 csi=00 siz=24 off=0
   kxsbbbfp=b6c9ea50  bln=24  avl=02  flg=05
   value=1
EXEC
#20:c=10000,e=83285,p=0,cr=0,cu=0,mis=1,r=0,dep=2,og=4,tim=1218601171720527
FETCH
#20:c=10000,e=10349,p=0,cr=4,cu=0,mis=0,r=1,dep=2,og=4,tim=1218601171730970
STAT #20 id=1 cnt=1 pid=0 pos=1 obj=18 op='TABLE ACCESS BY INDEX ROWID OBJ$
(cr=4 pr=0 pw=0 time=0 us cost=4 size=82 card=1)'
STAT #20 id=2 cnt=1 pid=1 pos=1 obj=37 op='INDEX RANGE SCAN I_OBJ2 (cr=3
pr=0 pw=0 time=0 us cost=3 size=0 card=1)'
=====================
PARSING IN CURSOR #12 len=23 dep=0 uid=0 oct=3 lid=0 tim=1218601479482076
hv=196595040 ad='278c37e0' sqlid='gtzdg685vgmb0'

select * from oe.orders

END OF STMT
PARSE
#12:c=50000,e=130822,p=3,cr=127,cu=0,mis=1,r=0,dep=0,og=1,tim=12186014794820
67
BINDS #12:
EXEC #12:c=0,e=41,p=0,cr=0,cu=0,mis=0,r=0,dep=0,og=1,tim=1218601479482192
WAIT #12: nam='SQL*Net message to client' ela= 9 driver id=1650815232
#bytes=1 p3=0 obj#=70320 tim=1218601479482254
WAIT #12: nam='db file sequential read' ela= 623 file#=5 block#=347 blocks=1
obj#=70309 tim=1218601479523634
WAIT #12: nam='db file scattered read' ela= 39197 file#=5 block#=348
blocks=5 obj#=70309 tim=1218601479563027
FETCH
#12:c=20000,e=45183,p=6,cr=6,cu=0,mis=0,r=1,dep=0,og=1,tim=1218601479568025
WAIT #12: nam='SQL*Net message from client' ela= 1102 driver id=1650815232
#bytes=1 p3=0 obj#=70309 tim=1218601479569404
WAIT #12: nam='SQL*Net message to client' ela= 6 driver id=1650815232
#bytes=1 p3=0 obj#=70309 tim=1218601479569531
FETCH #12:c=0,e=184,p=0,cr=1,cu=0,mis=0,r=15,dep=0,og=1,tim=1218601479569667
WAIT #12: nam='SQL*Net message from client' ela= 2104 driver id=1650815232
#bytes=1 p3=0 obj#=70309 tim=1218601479571820
=====================
PARSING IN CURSOR #34 len=25 dep=0 uid=0 oct=3 lid=0 tim=1218601171867798
hv=1015952610 ad='27891de8' sqlid='1mpqj84y8wd72'

select * from oe.products

END OF STMT
PARSE
#34:c=80000,e=234825,p=1,cr=140,cu=0,mis=1,r=0,dep=0,og=1,tim=12186011718677
86
BINDS #34:
EXEC #34:c=0,e=104,p=0,cr=0,cu=0,mis=0,r=0,dep=0,og=1,tim=1218601171867999
```

```
WAIT #34: nam='SQL*Net message to client' ela= 15 driver id=1650815232
#bytes=1 p3=0 obj#=70310 tim=1218601171868079
WAIT #34: nam='db file sequential read' ela= 62 file#=5 block#=379 blocks=1
obj#=70317 tim=1218601171868465
WAIT #34: nam='db file scattered read' ela= 25976 file#=5 block#=380
blocks=5 obj#=70317 tim=1218601171894737
WAIT #34: nam='db file scattered read' ela= 23554 file#=5 block#=705
blocks=8 obj#=70317 tim=1218601171926415
WAIT #34: nam='db file sequential read' ela= 189 file#=5 block#=395 blocks=1
obj#=70320 tim=1218601171929884
WAIT #34: nam='db file scattered read' ela= 789 file#=5 block#=396 blocks=5
obj#=70320 tim=1218601171930881
FETCH
#34:c=10000,e=63326,p=20,cr=20,cu=0,mis=0,r=1,dep=0,og=1,tim=121860117193148
0
WAIT #34: nam='SQL*Net message from client' ela= 82912 driver id=1650815232
#bytes=1 p3=0 obj#=70320 tim=1218601172014487
WAIT #34: nam='SQL*Net message to client' ela= 8 driver id=1650815232
#bytes=1 p3=0 obj#=70320 tim=1218601172014696
```

The above trace file is a raw data dump for SQL activities including wait events, cursor and other query activity. Since the volume of data is quite large and difficult to interpret and review for the raw trace file, view an example next using TKPROF to format the SQL trace file into a more readable format for analysis.

TKPROF

Oracle 11g provides yet another useful tool for tracing and tuning Oracle queries and session activity called TKPROF. TKPROF is the transient kernel profile utility available since version 7 of Oracle and provides formatting of trace files generated by other Oracle tools and activities such as dumps from Oradebug and SQL trace sessions.

What TKPROF provides is a user readable formatted text file for review and analysis. The nice thing about the TKPROF utility is that it allows for formatting trace files for focused data analysis critical for performance tuning and analysis. The DBA can dump all details for execution plans similar to that displayed by AutoTrace and explain as well as performance statistics for disk reads and system calls used by queries to be tuned. Of further note, TKPROF is an operating system utility independent of the Oracle database. As such, it is to be run from the operating system prompt and not within Oracle. To view the help options with TKPROF, simply enter the *tkprof* command with no options as shown below.

```
[oracle@raclinux1 trace]$ tkprof

Usage: tkprof tracefile outputfile [explain= ] [table= ]
              [print= ] [insert= ] [sys= ] [sort= ]
  table=schema.tablename   Use 'schema.tablename' with 'explain=' option.
  explain=user/password    Connect to ORACLE and issue EXPLAIN PLAN.
  print=integer      List only the first 'integer' SQL statements.
  aggregate=yes|no
  insert=filename  List SQL statements and data inside INSERT statements.
  sys=no           TKPROF does not list SQL statements run as user SYS.
  record=filename  Record non-recursive statements found in the trace file.
  waits=yes|no     Record summary for any wait events found in the trace
file.
  sort=option      Set of zero or more of the following sort options:
    prscnt   number of times parse was called
    prscpu   cpu time parsing
    prsela   elapsed time parsing
    prsdsk   number of disk reads during parse
    prsqry   number of buffers for consistent read during parse
    prscu    number of buffers for current read during parse
    prsmis   number of misses in library cache during parse
    execnt   number of execute was called
    execpu   cpu time spent executing
    exeela   elapsed time executing
    exedsk   number of disk reads during execute
    exeqry   number of buffers for consistent read during execute
    execu    number of buffers for current read during execute
    exerow   number of rows processed during execute
    exemis   number of library cache misses during execute
    fchcnt   number of times fetch was called
    fchcpu   cpu time spent fetching
    fchela   elapsed time fetching
    fchdsk   number of disk reads during fetch
    fchqry   number of buffers for consistent read during fetch
    fchcu    number of buffers for current read during fetch
    fchrow   number of rows fetched
    userid   userid of user that parsed the cursor
```

In order to use TKPROF, provide an input trace file generated from a previous Oracle 11g trace session, such as using SQL trace or Oradebug, and the output report file with the desired options for the trace report.

TKPROF Syntax

As mentioned previously, TKPROF is run from the operating system command shell prompt. The syntax for TKPROF is as follows:

```
tkprof input_trace_filename output_report_filename [waits=yes|no]
[sort=option] [print=n] [aggregate=yes|no] [insert=filename] [sys=yes|no]
[table=schema.table] [explain=user/password] [record=filename] [width=n]
```

An example of how to use TKPROF to output the complete execution plan and performance statistics from the recent SQL trace session is shown next.

```
[oracle@raclinux1 trace]$ tkprof ORA11G_ora_3945_10046_trace.trc
ora11gtrace_10046.rpt waits=yes aggregate=yes sys=yes explain=sys/oracle

TKPROF: Release 11.1.0.6.0 - Production on Wed Aug 13 01:28:00 2008

Copyright (c) 1982, 2007, Oracle.  All rights reserved.

[oracle@raclinux1 trace]$ view ora11gtrace_10046.rpt

TKPROF: Release 11.1.0.6.0 - Production on Wed Aug 13 01:28:00 2008
Copyright (c) 1982, 2007, Oracle.  All rights reserved.

Trace file: ORA11G_ora_3945_10046_trace.trc
Sort options: default

********************************************************************
count    = number of times OCI procedure was executed
cpu      = cpu time in seconds executing
elapsed  = elapsed time in seconds executing
disk     = number of physical reads of buffers from disk
query    = number of buffers gotten for consistent read
current  = number of buffers gotten in current mode (usually for update)
rows     = number of rows processed by the fetch or execute call
********************************************************************
SQL ID : 1mpqj84y8wd72
select *
from
 oe.products

call     count      cpu    elapsed      disk      query    current       rows
------- ------  -------- ---------- ---------- ---------- ---------- ----------
Parse        1     0.01       0.01          0          0          0          0
Execute      1     0.00       0.00          0          0          0          0
Fetch       21     0.08       0.33        385        410          0        288
------- ------  -------- ---------- ---------- ---------- ---------- ----------
total       23     0.09       0.35        385        410          0        288

Misses in library cache during parse: 1
Optimizer mode: ALL_ROWS
Parsing user id: SYS

Rows     Row Source Operation
-------  ---------------------------------------------------
    288   HASH JOIN OUTER (cr=410 pr=385 pw=385 time=18571 us cost=108
size=144864 card=288)
    288    TABLE ACCESS FULL PRODUCT_INFORMATION (cr=16 pr=14 pw=14
time=25509 us cost=5 size=63360 card=288)
    288    TABLE ACCESS FULL PRODUCT_DESCRIPTIONS (cr=394 pr=371 pw=371
time=14095 us cost=102 size=81504 card=288)

Elapsed times include waiting on following events:
```

Elapsed times include waiting on following events:

Event waited on	Times Waited	Max. Wait	Total Waited
SQL*Net message to client	21	0.00	0.00
db file sequential read	2	0.00	0.00
db file scattered read	22	0.06	0.21
SQL*Net message from client	21	148.92	155.68
SQL*Net more data to client	4	0.01	0.02

****

```
SQL ID : gtzdg685vgmb0
select *
from
 oe.orders
```

call	count	cpu	elapsed	disk	query	current	rows
Parse	1	0.02	0.03	0	0	0	0
Execute	1	0.00	0.00	0	0	0	0
Fetch	8	0.03	0.07	6	14	0	105
total	10	0.05	0.11	6	14	0	105

Misses in library cache during parse: 1
Optimizer mode: ALL_ROWS
Parsing user id: SYS

Rows	Row Source Operation
105	TABLE ACCESS FULL ORDERS (cr=14 pr=6 pw=6 time=21499 us cost=3 size=3885 card=105)

Elapsed times include waiting on following events:

Event waited on	Times Waited	Max. Wait	Total Waited ---
SQL*Net message to client	8	0.00	0.00
db file sequential read	1	0.00	0.00
db file scattered read	1	0.03	0.03
SQL*Net message from client	8	164.94	165.02

****

Elapsed times include waiting on following events:

Event waited on	Times Waited	Max. Wait	Total Waited
SQL*Net message to client	7	0.00	0.00
SQL*Net message from client	7	64.81	119.90
db file sequential read	4	0.04	0.06
SQL*Net break/reset to client	14	0.01	0.01

```
     29   user  SQL statements in session.
     87   internal SQL statements in session.
    116   SQL statements in session.
      0   statements explained in this session.
```

****

```
Trace file: ORA11G_ora_3945_10046_trace.trc
Trace file compatibility: 11.01.00
Sort options: default

      1   session in tracefile.
     29   user  SQL statements in trace file.
     87   internal SQL statements in trace file.
    116   SQL statements in trace file.
     34   unique SQL statements in trace file.
```

```
2295  lines in trace file.
 472  elapsed seconds in trace file.
```

The above TKPROF report shows a valuable report summary of crucial tuning and query statistics on how the SQL queries impact current database performance. In addition to the output from the explain plan and execution plans, there are also the wait events currently causing performance issues within the Oracle 11g database by the queries currently executing in the session or instance wide level. Next to be outlined is how to use the SQL tuning packages available with Oracle 11g.

SQL Tuning Packages for Oracle 11g

Oracle 11g builds upon the automatic SQL tuning advisors that were introduced in Oracle 10g. The new Automatic SQL Tuning Advisor with Oracle 11g provides automation for tuning inefficient SQL statements as well as providing SQL profile recommendations in the form of advisor output details from the SQL Tuning Advisor (STA). The *dbms_sqltune* package is used as the foundation for the automatic SQL tuning functions. Follow the next example illustrating how to use this new feature for Oracle 11g automatic SQL tuning. First, set up and grant the privileges and roles to the SH schema account so that the tuning session can be run.

```
[oracle@raclinux1 ~]$ sqlplus /nolog

SQL*Plus: Release 11.1.0.6.0 - Production on Thu Aug 14 12:57:59 2008

Copyright (c) 1982, 2007, Oracle.  All rights reserved.

SQL> connect /as sysdba
Connected.
SQL> grant advisor to sh;

Grant succeeded.
SQL> grant select_catalog_role to sh;

Grant succeeded.

SQL> grant execute on DBMS_SQLTUNE to sh;

Grant succeeded.
```

The next step is to create a PL/SQL script to use the *dbms_sqltune* package for the STA to tune a query for the SH schema. The SQL Tune Advisor uses tuning tasks to perform automatic SQL tuning for Oracle 11g queries. Below is the sample PL/SQL script for creating a new tuning task.

```
SQL> DECLARE
  2      sql_task_name VARCHAR2(30);
  3      tune_sqltext CLOB;
  4  BEGIN
  5      tune_sqltext :=' SELECT * ' ||
  6          'FROM sales '|| 'WHERE prod_id=20 AND '|| 'cust_id=200 ';
  7      sql_task_name := DBMS_SQLTUNE.CREATE_TUNING_TASK(
  8          sql_text=>tune_sqltext,
  9          user_name=>'SH',
 10          scope=>'COMPREHENSIVE',
 11          time_limit=>60,
 12          task_name=>'TUNE_SH_TASK',
 13          description=>'New task for tuning SH query');
 14  END;
 15  /

PL/SQL procedure successfully completed.
```

The *user_name* references the specific user schema for which the *create_tuning_task* function will tune the query. *Comprehensive* indicates that the tuning advisor will also perform SQL profile analysis in addition to tuning the query and, if desired, an additional optional parameter called *time_limit* can be used to specify the time allocated for performing the automatic tuning analysis. If the goal is to find the current tuning tasks for Oracle 11g database, issue the following query:

```
SQL> select task_name from dba_advisor_log
  2  where owner-'SH';

TASK_NAME
------------------------------
 Tune_SH_query_task
```

Now that the new tuning task is created for the SH schema and query, run the task to obtain the tuning recommendations.

```
SQL> begin
  2      DBMS_SQLTUNE.EXECUTE_TUNING_TASK(task_name=>' TUNE_SH_TASK');
  3  end;
  4  /
```

```
PL/SQL procedure successfully completed.
```

Another way to run the task is to use the following command:

```
SQL> execute dbms_sqltune.execute_tuning_task(task_name=>'TUNE_SH_TASK');

PL/SQL procedure successfully completed.
```

Now verify that the task ran successfully to completion:

```
SQL> select task_name, status, execution_start, execution_end
  2  from dba_advisor_log
  3  where owner='SH';

TASK_NAME                          STATUS       EXECUTION EXECUTION
-------------------------------    -----------  --------- ---------
 TUNE_SH_TASK                      COMPLETED    14-AUG-08 14-AUG-08
```

The last step is to view the SQL tuning advisor recommendations with the following example. Using the *report_tuning_task* function in the *dbms_sqltune* package, the advisor tuning report is shown below:

```
SQL> select dbms_sqltune.report_tuning_task('TUNE_SH_TASK')
  2  from dual;

DBMS_SQLTUNE.REPORT_TUNING_TASK('TUNE_SH_TASK')
-------------------------------------------------------------------
GENERAL INFORMATION SECTION
-------------------------------------------------------------------
Tuning Task Name                : TUNE_SH_TASK
Tuning Task Owner               : SH
Workload Type                   : Single SQL Statement
Scope                           : COMPREHENSIVE
Time Limit(seconds)             : 60
Completion Status               : COMPLETED
Started at                      : 08/14/2008 13:46:22
Completed at                    : 08/14/2008 13:46:23

DBMS_SQLTUNE.REPORT_TUNING_TASK('TUNE_SH_TASK')
-------------------------------------------------------------------
Schema Name: SH
SQL ID     : dbq1k7xwc387x
SQL Text   :   SELECT * FROM sales WHERE prod_id=20 AND cust_id=200

-----------------------------------------------------------------FINDINGS
SECTION (1 finding)
---------------------------------------------------------------1- Index
Finding (see explain plans section below)
```

Based on the report from the SQL Tuning Advisor, examine indexes on the table to improve query performance.

Oracle 11g provides additional useful views such as *dbms_sqltune _statistics*, *dbms_sqltune_binds* and *dbms_sqltune _plans* to analyze operation of the SQL tuning functions. To enable or disable automatic SQL tuning, the *dbms_auto_task_admin* package can be used with PL/SQL scripts for Oracle 11g.

Dbms_stats with Oracle 11g

Oracle 11g expands on the statistics reporting and collection mechanism available with the *dbms_stats* package in previous releases. Both system and database statistics can be collected and migrated between schemas and databases. Enhancements to the *dbms_stats* package in Oracle 11g include the new feature for extended statistics collection which allows the optimizer to gather statistics for correlated columns on tables as well as the mechanism for expression statistics with expression functions. In addition, Oracle 11g includes a new feature for *dbms_stats* to gather public and private statistics. Private statistics are statistics that have been collected but not advertised as used by the Cost Based Optimizer (CBO).

Oracle 11g has replaced the *get_param* function available with *dbms_stats* to return default values for parameters that are configured by default for the *dbms_stats* package. For sake of backward compatibility, the *get_param* function is still available in 11g for *dbms_stats* and is called with a query like:

```
SQL> select dbms_stats.get_param('PUBLISH') from dual;

DBMS_STATS.GET_PARAM('PUBLISH')
--------------------------------    --------------------------------TRUE
```

In Oracle 11g, the new function call to *dbms_stats* for managing default parameters is called via the *get_prefs* function to this package. For example, to show the default values for various preferences with *dbms_stats* in Oracle 11g, use this function with *dbms_stats* to obtain values for a single parameter such as that for *stale_percent* as shown below.

```
SQL> select dbms_stats.get_prefs('stale_percent','SH','products')
```

```
  2  stale_percent from dual;

STALE_PERCENT
---------------------------------------------------
10
```

Also set preferences for the *dbms_stats* collection of statistics for Oracle 11g using the *set_global_prefs* function which allows setting of global preferences for parameters associated with *dbms_stats*. For example, set statistics collection to 65%:

```
SQL> exec dbms_stats.set_global_prefs('estimate_percent','65');

PL/SQL procedure successfully completed.
```

After the *global_prefs* have been set to 65%, verify this with the below sample query:

```
SQL> select dbms_stats.get_prefs('estimate_percent','SCOTT','EMP')
estimate_percent from dual;

ESTIMATE_PERCENT
----------------------------------------------
65
```

It is also possible to export and import statistics preferences in Oracle 11g using the *export_database_prefs* and *import_database_prefs* functions available for *dbms_stats*.

Now take a look at how to collect and view statistics gathered with *dbms_stats* for column based statistics. The benefit of using the new multicolumn statistics collection option with *dbms_stats* and Oracle 11g is that performance collection statistics often are skewed incorrectly and the optimizer behaves incorrectly with Oracle when statistics are collected on only one table column. Multiple column based statistics collection improves optimizer query selection. An example of how to do this is explained with the following query for *dbms_stats*. This correlates nicely with the extended statistics feature new to Oracle 11g for *dbms_stats*. First, create a column group as follows for Oracle 11g:

```
SQL> var ret_col varchar2(2000)
SQL> exec :ret_col :=
dbms_stats.create_extended_stats('SH','PRODUCTS','(PROD_ID, PROD_NAME)');
```

```
PL/SQL procedure successfully completed.
SQL> print :ret_col

RET_COL
---------------------------------------------------------------------
SYS_STUQD09IA4IAL#B0JHHDVZCGIJ
```

Then collect extended statistics for multiple columns on the *sh.products* table.

```
SQL> begin
  2      dbms_stats.gather_table_stats(
  3          ownname=>'SH',
  4          tabname=>'PRODUCTS',
  5          estimate_percent=>100,
  6          method_opt=>'FOR ALL COLUMNS SIZE SKEWONLY FOR COLUMNS (PROD_ID,
PROD_NAME)',
  7          cascade=> true
  8  );
  9  end;
 10  /
```

After the extended column statistics are created and collected for the *products* table, query the *dba_stat_extensions* view to show the details for the new statistic extensions.

```
SQL> select owner, table_name, extension, extension_name
  2  from dba_stat_extensions
  3  where owner='SH';

OWNER                            TABLE_NAME
-----------------------------    ------------------------------
EXTENSION
---------------------------------------------------------------------
EXTENSION_NAME
-----------------------------
SH                               PRODUCTS
("PROD_ID","PROD_NAME")
SYS_STUQD09IA4IAL#B0JHHDVZCCIJ
```

For additional information on the use *dbms_stats*, please consult the Oracle 11g Performance Tuning Guide available online from the Oracle http://otn.oracle.com website.

Summary

In this chapter on performance tools for Oracle 11g, it was explained how to best leverage and implement some of the most useful

---

performance tools that are poorly documented or hidden within Oracle 11g. The review included the following points:

- Using AutoTrace
- Using SQL Trace for event-based monitoring and debugging
- TKPROF for trace file analysis
- SQL Tune packages review for Oracle 11g
- *Dbms_stats* for Oracle 11g

In the next chapter, the voyage will continue into debugging Oracle 11g issues with the Oradebug utility.

Using the Oradebug Utility for Oracle 11g

This chapter is about the powerful use of the poorly documented Oradebug utility. Many of the features and functions provided by this Oracle power tool to perform root cause problem analysis with Oracle 10g and 11g databases as well as monitoring and performance tuning tasks will be explored.

What is Oradebug?

There are many useful analysis and monitoring tools in the Oracle database environment for the database professional to review and tune database performance along with understanding general database health and status. However, not all of the tools are documented or supported by Oracle when a service call is opened via Oracle Metalink to resolve a difficult issue with the Oracle database.

Oradebug is one such utility that is poorly understood by most Oracle professionals. It is also not documented very well in the Oracle documentation with the scarce mention of it within a couple of old Metalink Support notes.

Yet when a difficult performance issue or database hang failure situation arises within the Oracle database environment, the Oradebug utility is extremely valuable. It is used to pinpoint the root cause of the problem when other tools fail to provide the required analysis of database internal issues. In this chapter, the details on how to use Oradebug in a wide variety of difficult Oracle database scenarios will be covered.

By learning how to tap into the power of this potent utility, the Oracle DBA will become an expert on resolving painful database hangs and performance issues and also gain an understanding on the core database internals for how the Oracle database engine really works. At the same time, prudent caution is to be exercised when using the various functions with the Oradebug utility because database corruption and/or database loss may occur if the DBA is careless when using the tool. The recommendation for Oracle professionals who wish to learn how to use the Oradebug utility is to first test it out in a sandbox or non-production database to avoid making any mistakes that could impact a live mission critical system.

New Features for Oradebug with Oracle 11g

Oradebug evolved from an earlier internal database diagnostic tool called ORADBX in the Oracle7 database release. Among the many functions possible with Oradebug are tracing of user sessions, dumping memory for the SGA with Oracle as well as the ability to stop and resume database processing and the analysis of SQL statements and core dump analysis.

Oracle 11g introduces new features with Oradebug in terms of events that can be monitored and traced. In particular, the new advisor events in 11g can now be traced and monitored by Oradebug, as can new memory features for Automatic Memory Management (AMM).

For example, the new health monitor 11g feature operation can be traced using Oradebug for Oracle 11g with the command:

```
SQL> Oradebug dump hm_fw_trace 3

Statement processed.
```

Tracing Errors with Oradebug

Oradebug is available for all database versions of Oracle starting with the Oracle7 release. This chapter will focus on examples from Oracle 10g on Windows and Oracle 11g on Red Hat Linux platforms in order to provide the latest features on how Oradebug works with current versions. In order to start a new session of the Oradebug utility, access to an Oracle database account with SYSDBA level privileges is required. Oradebug is invoked via the Oracle SQL*Plus interface.

When the Oradebug utility is used for all operations, by default it will output trace files to the Oracle *user_dump_dest* directory on the local filesystem. In order to find the current location for the *user_dump_dest* directory within SQL*Plus, the command below will display the current default location for these trace files generated by Oradebug.

```
SQL> show parameter user_dump

NAME                                 TYPE        VALUE
------------------------------------ ----------- --------------------
user_dump_dest                       string
/u01/app/oracle/diag/rdbms/ora
                                                 11g/ORA11G/trace
```

Now take a look at how the location for the trace files is stored on Windows with Oracle 10g.

```
SQL> show parameter user_dump

NAME                                 TYPE        VALUE
------------------------------------ ----------- --------------------
user_dump_dest                       string
C:\ORACLE\PRODUCT\10.2.0\ADMIN
                                                 \APEX\UDUMP
```

Another way to display the location for current trace files generated with Oradebug is via the Oradebug *tracefile_name* command.

```
SQL> Oradebug tracefile_name

/u01/app/oracle/diag/rdbms/ora11g/ORA11G/trace/ORA11G_ora_15527.trc
```

Next are the basic requirements to configure Oracle for use with Oradebug. There are two ways to use the Oradebug utility when tuning or diagnosing Oracle database issues. The first method is to configure Oradebug to use a specific Oracle user process or SPID (Service Profile Identifier) for analysis. The second method to set up Oradebug for analysis and troubleshooting for Oracle related issues is to use the current logged in session or SPID.

First to be reviewed is the procedure to trace a specific process in Oracle with Oradebug. Find out what the specific process ID is within Oracle. To do this, run the following example query using the *v$session* and *v$process* performance views:

```
Connected to:
Oracle Database 11g Enterprise Edition Release 11.1.0.6.0 - Production
With the Partitioning, OLAP, Data Mining and Real Application Testing
options

SQL> select s.username, s.sid, p.spid
  2  from v$session s, v$process p
  3  where s.paddr=p.addr;
```

USERNAME	SID	SPID
	169	7955
	168	7957
	166	7961
	167	7963
	165	7965
	158	7975
	162	7969
	163	7971
	164	7973
	161	7977
	160	7979
	159	7981
	156	7983
	157	7985
	152	8067
	153	8022
SYS	155	8065
	151	8069
	150	8071
USERNAME	SID	SPID
	149	8073
	145	8075
	142	8087
	141	8100
	132	9448
	136	8108
	135	8145
	154	8695
	123	22719
SCOTT	127	22428
SYS	126	22497

```
30 rows selected.
```

The results of the above query provide the DBA with the SPID that will be needed to trace a particular session with Oradebug. If there is a specific user in mind, simply plug in the username in the above query to retrieve more fine-grained results such as the query below:

```
SQL> select s.username, s.sid, p.spid
  2  from v$session s, v$process p
  3  where s.paddr=p.addr
  4  and s.username='SCOTT';

USERNAME                              SID SPID
------------------------------ ---------- ------------------------
SCOTT                                 127 22428
```

Now that results are received from the previous queries to find the SPID details, plug these values into Oradebug to initialize a new trace session. The first method for a new trace with Oradebug involves the currently logged in session to trace Oracle activities using the *setmypid* command within Oradebug as shown next.

```
[oracle@raclinux1 ~]$ sqlplus "/as sysdba"
SQL*Plus: Release 11.1.0.6.0 - Production on Wed Jul 23 18:02:51 2008
Copyright (c) 1982, 2007, Oracle.  All rights reserved.

Connected to:
Oracle Database 11g Enterprise Edition Release 11.1.0.6.0 - Production
With the Partitioning, OLAP, Data Mining and Real Application Testing
options

SQL> Oradebug setmypid

Statement processed.
```

Conversely, the exact SPID identifier that was obtained from the earlier query can be used to trace the session for the user SCOTT logged into the Oracle 11g database as shown below.

```
[oracle@raclinux1 ~]$ sqlplus "/as sysdba"

SQL*Plus: Release 11.1.0.6.0 - Production on Wed Jul 23 18:05:33 2008

Copyright (c) 1982, 2007, Oracle.  All rights reserved.

Connected to:
Oracle Database 11g Enterprise Edition Release 11.1.0.6.0 - Production
With the Partitioning, OLAP, Data Mining and Real Application Testing
options

SQL> Oradebug setospid 22428
```

```
Oracle pid: 32, Unix process pid: 22428, image:
oracle@raclinux1.us.oracle.com ( TNS V1-V3)
```

The syntax for using the *setospid* option with Oradebug is as follows:

```
Oradebug setospid <SPID>
```

Now that configuring the user session with Oradebug has been illustrated, allow the trace file to grow without limit so that all details can be collected without errors when using Oradebug. Oradebug has an option called unlimit which frees the trace file from size restriction. The following example shows how to use the unlimit option with Oradebug so that there is no size restriction on the trace file generated by Oradebug trace activity.

```
SQL> Oradebug unlimit

Statement processed.
```

As a side note, the dump file size is controlled by the *max_dump_file_size* parameter within the Oracle initialization parameter file as shown in the following example.

```
SQL> show parameter max_dump

NAME                                 TYPE        VALUE
------------------------------------ ----------- -------------------
max_dump_file_size                   string      unlimited
```

Now that Oradebug has been set up for the initial trace session, next to be shown are the trace file contents.

```
SQL> Oradebug tracefile_name

/u01/app/oracle/diag/rdbms/ora11g/ORA11G/trace/ORA11G_ora_22428.trc
SQL> !view
/u01/app/oracle/diag/rdbms/ora11g/ORA11G/trace/ORA11G_ora_22428.trc

Trace file
/u01/app/oracle/diag/rdbms/ora11g/ORA11G/trace/ORA11G_ora_22428.trc
Oracle Database 11g Enterprise Edition Release 11.1.0.6.0 - Production
With the Partitioning, OLAP, Data Mining and Real Application Testing
options
ORACLE_HOME = /u01/app/oracle/product/10.2.0/db_1
System name:    Linux
Node name:      raclinux1.us.oracle.com
```

```
Release:        2.6.9-5.EL
Version:        #1 Sun Jun 12 12:31:23 IDT 2005
Machine:        i686
Instance name: ORA11G
Redo thread mounted by this instance: 1
Oracle process number: 32
Unix process pid: 22428, image: oracle@raclinux1.us.oracle.com (TNS V1-V3)

*** 2008-07-23 18:15:12.071
*** SESSION ID:(127.548) 2008-07-23 18:15:12.071
*** CLIENT ID:() 2008-07-23 18:15:12.071
*** SERVICE NAME:(SYS$USERS) 2008-07-23 18:15:12.071
*** MODULE NAME:(SQL*Plus) 2008-07-23 18:15:12.071
*** ACTION NAME:() 2008-07-23 18:15:12.071
```

To end a trace session for Oradebug, use the Oradebug *close_trace* command which tells Oracle to stop writing trace files to the current session. This is useful in the event that one wishes to continue using Oracle with the current session after using Oradebug. Since no significant activity has been performed yet within the Oracle database for the SCOTT user, not much information is contained within the trace file from the initial session. Also, do not use the semicolon (;) to terminate commands with Oradebug; otherwise, a syntax error will be received.

So far, the initial steps for using Oradebug have been covered. Next are some examples of how to trace errors with Oracle 11g using Oradebug.

The actual syntax for tracing errors in Oracle 11g is shown in the following command:

```
Oradebug event <error_code> trace name errorstack level <level>
```

Once the security identifier (SID) that is to be monitored is set, to trace an error is quite easy. To trace a specific error in Oracle 11g, input the actual error code to the event command for the utility. For instance, if the wish is to trace all ORA-04030 ("Out of Process Memory") errors in Oracle 11g, issue the following command for Oradebug:

```
SQL> Oradebug event 04030 trace name errorstack level 3

Statement processed.
```

> Note: This will only generate a message in the Oradebug trace file if this error occurs within the Oracle 11g database.

In the trace file, the commands issued earlier are:

```
*** 2008-08-15 15:14:42.728
Oradebug command 'setmypid' console output: <none>
*** 2008-08-15 15:14:59.476
Processing Oradebug command 'event 04030 trace name errorstack level 3'
```

Once the trace files have been generated for Oradebug, either view the raw trace file or use the utility TKPROF to format the trace file into an easier format for analysis. It really depends on for what purpose Oradebug is being used. If it is to just look at performance results for tuning, TKPROF does an excellent job for formatting the trace dump into a more readable format. For memory dumps and core dumps, viewing the raw trace file is advised.

Using Oradebug to Determine the Events Set in Oracle 11g

Oradebug has the ability to set many different database tracing events for Oracle 11g. Common events that can be set for Oracle 11g for tracing are 10053 for the Oracle 11g Cost Based Optimizer (CBO) as well as SQL trace event 10046.

In addition to these events, Oradebug can perform tracing at many different levels of detail. The following event levels are possible for Oradebug:

- **Level 1:** contains the basic level of trace information. For example, this trace level will display the bind variables in PL/SQL and SQL statements.

- **Level 8:** provides the trace details from Level 1 plus the wait events for elapsed times that are more than current CPU timings.

- **Level 12:** adds in all the previous trace level information in addition to all wait event information.

To view events in use, simply open and view the corresponding trace file generated by Oradebug. All events will be listed in the trace file that are processed and monitored by Oradebug and Oracle 11g.

To dump the events in use with releases before Oracle 11g, the following command can be used:

```
Oradebug dump events <event_type>
```

Oracle has three main types of events that can be dumped with Oradebug:

- Session event has the associated ID of 1

- Process event has the associated ID of 2

- System event has the associated ID of 4

To dump system events, issue the following command:

```
Oradebug dump events <event id>
```

The following figure illustrates how to determine events set for an Oracle 10g database.

```
C:\oracle>sqlplus /nolog

SQL*Plus: Release 10.1.0.3.0 - Production on Fri Aug 15 17:05:55 2008

Copyright (c) 1982, 2004, Oracle.  All rights reserved.

SQL> Oradebug dump events 4

Statement processed.
Dump file c:\oracle\product\10.2.0\admin\orcl\udump\orcl_ora_2300.trc
Fri Aug 15 17:06:28 2008
ORACLE V10.2.0.1.0 - Production vsnsta=0
vsnsql=14 vsnxtr=3
Oracle Database 10g Enterprise Edition Release 10.2.0.1.0 - Production
With the Partitioning, OLAP and Data Mining options
Windows XP Version V5.1 Service Pack 2
CPU                 : 2 - type 586
Process Affinity    : 0x00000000
Memory (Avail/Total): Ph:591M/2037M, Ph+PgF:2412M/3933M, VA:1007M/2047M
Instance name: orcl

Redo thread mounted by this instance: 1
```

```
Oracle process number: 18

Windows thread id: 2300, image: ORACLE.EXE (SHAD)

*** 2008-08-15 17:06:29.421
*** SERVICE NAME:(SYS$USERS) 2008-08-15 17:06:28.562
*** SESSION ID:(155.3) 2008-08-15 17:06:28.562
Dump event group for level SYSTEM
TC Addr  Evt#(b10)   Action   TR Addr    Arm    Life
```

Now an example of how to determine events for processes in Oracle 10g using Oradebug is shown:

```
SQL> Oradebug dump events 2

Statement processed.
SQL> Oradebug tracefile_name
c:\oracle\product\10.2.0\admin\orcl\udump\orcl_ora_2300.trc

*** 2008-08-15 17:27:22.875
Dump event group for level PROCESS
TC Addr  Evt#(b10)   Action   TR Addr    Arm    Life
```

To determine events for sessions using Oradebug for Oracle 10g, issue the following command:

```
SQL> Oradebug dump events 1

Statement processed.
SQL> Oradebug tracefile_name
c:\oracle\product\10.2.0\admin\orcl\udump\orcl_ora_2300.trc
*** 2008-08-15 17:30:29.781
Dump event group for level SESSION
TC Addr  Evt#(b10)   Action   TR Addr    Arm    Life
```

Note: Oracle 11g no longer has the command *oradebug dump events* that was available with previous releases of Oracle. So in order to dump the events for Oracle 11g, the *dbms_system* package can be used instead of Oradebug for Oracle 11g release. A sample PL/SQL script is listed below in the code example to illustrate how to perform this task using the undocumented *read_ev* function call to *dbms_system*.

Connected to:

```
Oracle Database 11g Enterprise Edition Release 11.1.0.6.0 - Production
With the Partitioning, OLAP, Data Mining and Real Application Testing
options
```

```
SQL> set serveroutput on
SQL> declare
  2     event_level number;
  3   begin
  4     for i in 10000..10999 loop
  5     sys.dbms_system.read_ev(i,event_level);
  6     if (event_level > 0) then
  7       dbms_output.put_line('Event  '||to_char(i)||' set at level '||
  8             to_char(event_level));
  9     end if;
 10   end loop;
 11   end;
 12   /
```

PL/SQL procedure successfully completed.

Now save the above PL/SQL script as *check_events.sql*. Run these commands to set the following events:

```
SQL> alter session set sql_trace=true;
SQL> alter session set events '10015 trace name context forever, level 3';

SQL> @check_events.sql
Event  10015 set at level 3
```

PL/SQL procedure successfully completed.

Viewing Oracle RAC Events with Oradebug

Oradebug has the added features to trace and monitor all of the critical items for Oracle RAC environments including the ability to monitor and trace the Oracle RAC Clusterware (CRS) stack and Oracle 11g RAC interconnect operations for IPC (interprocess communications) usage as well.

Next to be covered is how to trace interconnect activities for Oracle 10g/11g RAC environments. Then how to trace Oracle RAC cluster operations for the Oracle RAC Clusterware stack as well as for the Oracle RAC cluster registry (OCR) and Oracle Cluster Synchronization Services (CSS) processes using Oradebug will be explained.

For tracing the interconnect with Oracle RAC, the following command would be issued:

```
Oradebug ipc
```

An example of how to use Oradebug to trace the interconnect and IPC activities is shown below:

```
[oracle@raclinux1 ~]$ sqlplus "/as sysdba"

SQL*Plus: Release 10.2.0.1.0 - Production on Fri Aug 15 21:43:46 2008

Copyright (c) 1982, 2005, Oracle.  All rights reserved.


Connected to:
Oracle Database 10g Enterprise Edition Release 10.2.0.1.0 - Production
With the Partitioning, Real Application Clusters, Oracle Label Security,
OLAP
and Data Mining Scoring Engine options

SQL> Oradebug setmypid

Statement processed.

SQL> Oradebug unlimit

Statement processed.

SQL> Oradebug ipc

Information written to trace file.

SQL> Oradebug tracefile_name

/u01/app/oracle/admin/RACDB/udump/racdb1_ora_6391.trc

SQL>

[oracle@raclinux1 ~]$ cd /u01/app/oracle/admin/RACDB/udump
[oracle@raclinux1 udump]$ view racdb1_ora_6391.trc
/u01/app/oracle/admin/RACDB/udump/racdb1_ora_6391.trc
Oracle Database 10g Enterprise Edition Release 10.2.0.1.0 - Production
With the Partitioning, Real Application Clusters, Oracle Label Security,
OLAP
and Data Mining Scoring Engine options
ORACLE_HOME = /u01/app/oracle/product/10.2.0/db_1
System name:    Linux
Node name:      raclinux1.us.oracle.com
Release:        2.6.9-5.EL
Version:        #1 Sun Jun 12 12:31:23 IDT 2005
Machine:        i686
Instance name: RACDB1
Redo thread mounted by this instance: 1
Oracle process number: 20
Unix process pid: 6391, image: oracle@raclinux1.us.oracle.com (TNS V1-V3)
system cpu time since last wait 0 sec 0 ticks
locked 1
blocked 0
timed wait receives 0
admno 0x769fcb68 admport:
SSKGXPT 0xcc75e9c flags SSKGXPT_READPENDING      info for network 0
```

```
        socket no 7      IP 10.10.10.11  UDP 2247
        sflags SSKGXPT_UP
        info for network 1
        socket no 0      IP 0.0.0.0      UDP 0
        sflags SSKGXPT_DOWN
        active 0         actcnt 1
context timestamp 0
        no ports
   sconno     accono   ertt  state   seq#   sent  async   sync rtrans
acks
```

To obtain a trace for Oracle RAC Clusterware, issue the following command:

```
Oradebug dump crs 3
```

To trace operations for the Oracle RAC cluster synchronization (CSS) operations, use the following command for Oradebug:

```
Oradebug dump css 3
```

To obtain a trace for the OCR with Oracle RAC, issue the following command:

```
Oradebug dump ocr 3
```

Now that key methods to debug and trace events for Oracle RAC using Oradebug have been explained, next to be shown are the methods to trace and debug memory for Oracle 11g.

Dumping Memory with Oradebug

One of the most powerful features available with the Oradebug utility for Oracle 11g is the ability to view memory structures via dump commands in Oradebug for database internals. To use these dump commands, obtain a helpful list with the Oradebug *dumplist* command as shown below.

```
[oracle@raclinux1 trace]$ sqlplus "/as sysdba"

SQL*Plus: Release 11.1.0.6.0 - Production on Fri Aug 15 18:56:22 2008

Copyright (c) 1982, 2007, Oracle.  All rights reserved.
```

```
Connected to:
Oracle Database 11g Enterprise Edition Release 11.1.0.6.0 - Production
With the Partitioning, OLAP, Data Mining and Real Application Testing
options

SQL> Oradebug dumplist

TRACE_BUFFER_ON
TRACE_BUFFER_OFF
LATCHES
PROCESSSTATE
SYSTEMSTATE
INSTANTIATIONSTATE
REFRESH_OS_STATS
CROSSIC
CONTEXTAREA
HANGDIAG_HEADER
HEAPDUMP
HEAPDUMP_ADDR
POKE_ADDRESS
POKE_LENGTH
POKE_VALUE
POKE_VALUE0
GLOBAL_AREA
REALFREEDUMP
FLUSH_JAVA_POOL
POOL_SIMULATOR
PGA_DETAIL_GET
PGA_DETAIL_DUMP
PGA_DETAIL_CANCEL
MODIFIED_PARAMETERS
EVENT_TSM_TEST
ERRORSTACK
CALLSTACK
TEST_STACK_DUMP
TEST_GET_CALLER
RECORD_CALLSTACK
EXCEPTION_DUMP
BG_MESSAGES
ENQUEUES
KSTDUMPCURPROC
KSTDUMPALLPROCS
KSTDUMPALLPROCS_CLUSTER
SIMULATE_EOV
KSFQP_LIMIT
KSKDUMPTRACE
DBSCHEDULER
LDAP_USER_DUMP
LDAP_KERNEL_DUMP
DUMP_ALL_OBJSTATS
DUMPGLOBALDATA
HANGANALYZE
HANGANALYZE_PROC
HANGANALYZE_GLOBAL
GES_STATE
OCR
CSS
CRS
SYSTEMSTATE_GLOBAL
```

```
MMAN_ALLOC_MEMORY
MMAN_CREATE_DEF_REQUEST
MMAN_CREATE_IMM_REQUEST
MMAN_IMM_REQUEST
DUMP_ALL_COMP_GRANULE_ADDRS
DUMP_ALL_COMP_GRANULES
DUMP_ALL_REQS
DUMP_TRANSFER_OPS
DUMP_ADV_SNAPSHOTS
ADJUST_SCN
NEXT_SCN_WRAP
CONTROLF
FLUSH_CACHE
FULL_DUMPS
BUFFERS
RECOVERY
SET_TSN_P1
BUFFER
PIN_BLOCKS
BC_SANITY_CHECK
PIN_RANDOM_BLOCKS
SET_NBLOCKS
CHECK_ROREUSE_SANITY
DUMP_PINNED_BUFFER_HISTORY
KCBO_OBJ_CHECK_DUMP
REDOLOGS
LOGHIST
ARCHIVE_ERROR
REDOHDR
LOGERROR
OPEN_FILES
DATA_ERR_ON
DATA_ERR_OFF
BLK0_FMTCHG
UPDATE_BLOCK0_FORMAT
TR_SET_BLOCK
TR_SET_ALL_BLOCKS
TR_SET_SIDE
TR_CRASH_AFTER_WRITE
TR_READ_ONE_SIDE
TR_CORRUPT_ONE_SIDE
TR_RESET_NORMAL
TEST_DB_ROBUSTNESS
LOCKS
GC_ELEMENTS
FILE_HDRS
KRB_CORRUPT_INTERVAL
KRB_CORRUPT_SIZE
KRB_CORRUPT_REPEAT
KRB_PIECE_FAIL
KRB_OPTIONS
KRB_FAIL_INPUT_FILENO
KRB_SIMULATE_NODE_AFFINITY
KRB_TRACE
KRB_BSET_DAYS
KRB_SET_TIME_SWITCH
KRB_OVERWRITE_ACTION
KRB_CORRUPT_SPHEADER_INTERVAL
KRB_CORRUPT_SPHEADER_REPEAT
```

```
KRB_CORRUPT_SPBITMAP_INTERVAL
KRB_CORRUPT_SPBITMAP_REPEAT
KRB_CORRUPT_SPBAD_INTERVAL
KRB_CORRUPT_SPBAD_REPEAT
KRB_UNUSED_OPTION
KRBMRSR_LIMIT
KRBMROR_LIMIT
KRC_TRACE
KRA_OPTIONS
KRA_TRACE
FBTAIL
FBINC
FBHDR
FLASHBACK_GEN
KTPR_DEBUG
DUMP_TEMP
DROP_SEGMENTS
TEST_SPACEBG
TREEDUMP
LONGF_CREATE
KDLIDMP
ROW_CACHE
LIBRARY_CACHE
CURSORDUMP
CURSORTRACE
CURSOR_STATS
SHARED_SERVER_STATE
JAVAINFO
KXFPCLEARSTATS
KXFPDUMPTRACE
KXFPBLATCHTEST
KXFXSLAVESTATE
KXFXCURSORSTATE
WORKAREATAB_DUMP
KUPPLATCHTEST
OBJECT_CACHE
SAVEPOINTS
RULESETDUMP
RULESETDUMP_ADDR
FAILOVER
OLAP_DUMP
SELFTESTASM
IOERREMUL
IOERREMULRNG
ALRT_TEST
AWR_TEST
AWR_FLUSH_TABLE_ON
AWR_FLUSH_TABLE_OFF
ASHDUMP
MMON_TEST
ATSK_TEST
HM_FW_TRACE
IR_FW_TRACE
KSDTRADV_TEST
SQL>
```

All of the new features in Oracle 11g can be traced now with the Oradebug utility such as the new health monitor and automatic diagnostic repository activities.

Dumping SGA Memory for Oracle 11g with Oradebug

Oradebug provides functions to dump all memory buffers and components for Oracle 11g and previous releases for the SGA. The Oradebug command *dumpsga* will output contents of the SGA for Oracle 11g to the trace file. This feature is especially useful when debugging memory leak problems with Oracle and working with senior internal Oracle support engineers to pinpoint the source of the memory problem at the Oracle kernel level.

The following example shows how to dump the SGA for Oracle 11g.

```
[oracle@raclinux1 trace]$ sqlplus "/as sysdba"

SQL*Plus: Release 11.1.0.6.0 - Production on Sat Aug 16 00:08:22 2008

Copyright (c) 1982, 2007, Oracle.  All rights reserved.


Connected to:
Oracle Database 11g Enterprise Edition Release 11.1.0.6.0 - Production
With the Partitioning, OLAP, Data Mining and Real Application Testing
options

SQL> Oradebug setmypid

Statement processed.

SQL> Oradebug unlimit

Statement processed.

SQL> Oradebug dumpsga

Statement processed.

SQL> Oradebug tracefile_name
/u01/app/oracle/diag/rdbms/ora11g/ORA11G/trace/ORA11G_ora_21292.trc
SQL> exit

Disconnected from Oracle Database 11g Enterprise Edition Release 11.1.0.6.0
- Production
With the Partitioning, OLAP, Data Mining and Real Application Testing
options
[oracle@raclinux1 trace]$ view ORA11G_ora_21292.trc
```

```
Trace file
/u01/app/oracle/diag/rdbms/ora11g/ORA11G/trace/ORA11G_ora_21292.trc
Oracle Database 11g Enterprise Edition Release 11.1.0.6.0 - Production
With the Partitioning, OLAP, Data Mining and Real Application Testing
options
ORACLE_HOME = /u01/app/oracle/product/11.1.0/11g
System name:    Linux
Node name:      raclinux1.us.oracle.com
Release:        2.6.9-5.EL
Version:        #1 Sun Jun 12 12:31:23 IDT 2005
Machine:        i686
Instance name: ORA11G
Redo thread mounted by this instance: 1
Oracle process number: 27
Unix process pid: 21292, image: oracle@raclinux1.us.oracle.com (TNS V1-V3)

*** 2008-08-16 00:08:30.647
*** SESSION ID:(127.45) 2008-08-16 00:08:30.647
*** CLIENT ID:() 2008-08-16 00:08:30.647
*** SERVICE NAME:(SYS$USERS) 2008-08-16 00:08:30.647
*** MODULE NAME:(sqlplus@raclinux1.us.oracle.com (TNS V1-V3)) 2008-08-16
00:08:30.647
*** ACTION NAME:() 2008-08-16 00:08:30.647
*** 2008-08-16 00:08:43.464

----- Fixed Areas Dump (level=2) -----
----- Dump of the Fixed SGA -----
ksmsgft ksmsgf_ [20000000, 20001000) = 00000000 00000000 00000000 00000000
...
Dump of memory from 0x20000010 to 0x20001000
20000010 00000000 00000000 00000000 00000000  [................]
   Repeat 254 times
kywmr * kywmrsga_ [20001000, 20001004) = 37834020
ksllt kywmll_ [20001004, 20001068) = 00000000 00000000 00000000 00000000 ...
Dump of memory from 0x20001014 to 0x20001068
20001010          00000000 00000000 00000000     [...........]
20001020 00000000 00000000 00000000 00000000  [................]
       Repeat 1 times
20001040 20001040 20001040 20001048 20001048  [@.. @.. H.. H.. ]
20001050 00000000 00000000 00000000 00000000  [................]
20001060 00000000 00000000                     [........]
ub4 kywmpleq_ [20001068, 2000106C) = 00000001
ub4 kywmpleq1_ [2000106C, 20001070) = 00000001
sword kywmpleq1_e_ [20001070, 20001074) = 0000014B
sword kywmwrm_ [20001074, 20001078) = 00000001
ub1 kywmplop_ [20001078, 2000107C) = 00000000
sword ksmvsg_ [2000107C, 20001080) = 00000EEE
```

One item of note is that the Oradebug *unlimit* command may be used before initiating memory dumps as these can grow quite large and exceed the default limit during a trace session. Next to be explored is how to view the library cache.

Using Oradebug to Examine the Library Cache State for Oracle 11g

As mentioned earlier, Oradebug has the dump function to report status and details of the Oracle 11g memory structures and buffers. For example, to examine the library cache for Oracle 11g, issue the following command:

```
Oradebug dump library_cache <level>
```

Now here is an example of how it works:

```
SQL> Oradebug dump library_cache 3

Statement processed.

SQL> exit

Disconnected from Oracle Database 11g Enterprise Edition Release 11.1.0.6.0
- Production
With the Partitioning, OLAP, Data Mining and Real Application Testing
options
[oracle@raclinux1 trace]$ view ORA11G_ora_10951.trc

Trace file
/u01/app/oracle/diag/rdbms/ora11g/ORA11G/trace/ORA11G_ora_10951.trc
Oracle Database 11g Enterprise Edition Release 11.1.0.6.0 - Production
With the Partitioning, OLAP, Data Mining and Real Application Testing
options
ORACLE_HOME = /u01/app/oracle/product/11.1.0/11g
System name:    Linux
Node name:      raclinux1.us.oracle.com
Release:        2.6.9-5.EL
Version:        #1 Sun Jun 12 12:31:23 IDT 2005
Machine:        i686
Instance name: ORA11G
Redo thread mounted by this instance: 1
Oracle process number: 18
Unix process pid: 10951, image: oracle@raclinux1.us.oracle.com (TNS V1-V3)

*** 2008-08-15 18:44:31.560
*** SESSION ID:(140.150) 2008-08-15 18:44:31.560
*** CLIENT ID:() 2008-08-15 18:44:31.560
*** SERVICE NAME:(SYS$USERS) 2008-08-15 18:44:31.560
*** MODULE NAME:(sqlplus@raclinux1.us.oracle.com (TNS V1-V3)) 2008-08-15
18:44:31.560
*** ACTION NAME:() 2008-08-15 18:44:31.560

*** 2008-08-15 18:48:05.175
Processing Oradebug command 'dump library_cache 3'
LIBRARY CACHE STATISTICS:
```

namespace	gets	hit ratio	pins	hit ratio	reloads	invalids
CRSR	21672	0.491	278408	0.913	6253	257
TABL	80413	0.938	103918	0.900	2686	0
BODY	6702	0.865	9143	0.898	16	0
TRGR	249	0.610	511	0.624	0	0
INDX	121	0.488	84	0.036	19	0
CLST	7303	0.998	4593	0.996	1	0
KGLT	0	0.000	0	0.000	0	0
PIPE	0	0.000	0	0.000	0	0
LOB	0	0.000	0	0.000	0	0
DIR	0	0.000	0	0.000	0	0
QUEU	3546	0.999	3546	0.997	1	0
OBJG	0	0.000	0	0.000	0	0
PROP	0	0.000	0	0.000	0	0
JVSC	0	0.000	0	0.000	0	0
JVRE	0	0.000	0	0.000	0	0
ROBJ	0	0.000	0	0.000	0	0
REIP	0	0.000	0	0.000	0	0
CPOB	0	0.000	0	0.000	0	0
EVNT	664	0.985	664	0.976	6	0
SUMM	0	0.000	0	0.000	0	0
DIMN	0	0.000	0	0.000	0	0
CTX	94	0.957	94	0.957	0	0
OUTL	0	0.000	0	0.000	0	0
RULS	10	0.900	10	0.700	2	0
RMGR	49	0.878	52	0.846	0	0
XDBS	0	0.000	0	0.000	0	0
PPLN	0	0.000	0	0.000	0	0
PCLS	0	0.000	0	0.000	0	0
SUBS	327	0.979	327	0.979	0	0
LOCS	0	0.000	0	0.000	0	0
RMOB	0	0.000	0	0.000	0	0
RSMD	0	0.000	0	0.000	0	0
JVSD	12	0.750	874	0.993	0	0
STFG	0	0.000	0	0.000	0	0
TRANS	0	0.000	0	0.000	0	0
RELC	0	0.000	0	0.000	0	0
RULE	0	0.000	0	0.000	0	0
STRM	0	0.000	0	0.000	0	0
REVC	3	0.333	0	0.000	0	0
STAP	0	0.000	0	0.000	0	0
RELS	0	0.000	0	0.000	0	0
RELD	0	0.000	0	0.000	0	0
IFSD	0	0.000	0	0.000	0	0
XDBC	0	0.000	0	0.000	0	0
USAG	0	0.000	0	0.000	0	0
MVOBTBL	41	0.537	41	0.512	1	0
JSQI	0	0.000	0	0.000	0	0
CDC	0	0.000	0	0.000	0	0
MVOBIND	43	0.535	43	0.512	1	0
STBO	0	0.000	0	0.000	0	0
HTSO	0	0.000	0	0.000	0	0
JSGA	5287	0.995	5287	0.995	0	0
JSET	1312	0.987	1309	0.746	315	0
TABL_T	0	0.000	0	0.000	0	0
CLST_T	0	0.000	0	0.000	0	0
INDX_T	0	0.000	0	0.000	0	0
NSCPD	0	0.000	0	0.000	0	0
JSLV	0	0.000	0	0.000	0	0
MODL	0	0.000	0	0.000	0	0
NSSC	0	0.000	0	0.000	0	0
LWTS	0	0.000	0	0.000	0	0
NDSD	0	0.000	0	0.000	0	0
XSSC	0	0.000	0	0.000	0	0
XDBZ	0	0.000	0	0.000	0	0
APPE	11969	0.998	12298	0.998	0	0
JSLJ	0	0.000	0	0.000	0	0
ROSR	0	0.000	0	0.000	0	0
SPRP	0	0.000	0	0.000	0	0
CUMULATIVE	139817	0.876	421202	0.914	9301	257

```
SGA:0x35a63ff8 flg = 87 dlfg = 0
LIBRARY CACHE HASH TABLE: size=131072 count=11851
Buckets with more than 20 objects:
```

```
NONE
Hash Chain Size      Number of Buckets
---------------      -----------------
             0                 119769
             1                  10768
             2                    523
             3                     11
             4                      1
             5                      0
             6                      0
             7                      0
             8                      0
             9                      0
            10                      0
            11                      0
            12                      0
            13                      0
            14                      0
            15                      0
            16                      0
            17                      0
            18                      0
            19                      0
```

Now that how to obtain memory traces and dumps for the SGA structures with Oracle 11g has been covered, obtaining a trace and memory dump for the Oracle 11g PGA memory structures will be displayed next.

Dumping PGA Memory for Oracle 11g Using Oradebug

In addition to obtaining a memory dump for the SGA and library cache, memory can also be dumped for the Oracle 11g PGA. To do this, use the following command:

```
Oradebug dump pga_detail_dump <level>
```

Here is an example of how to take a trace and dump of the PGA for Oracle 11g:

```
SQL> Oradebug setmypid

Statement processed.

SQL> Oradebug dump pga_detail_dump 3

Statement processed.

SQL> Oradebug tracefile_name
```

```
/u01/app/oracle/diag/rdbms/ora11g/ORA11G/trace/ORA11G_ora_23940.trc

*** 2008-08-16 00:30:08.239
Processing Oradebug command 'dump pga_detail_dump 3'
============================
Begin PGA memory detail dump
============================

*** 2008-08-16 00:30:08.730
=================================================
PGA memory detail for pid 3, OS pid 4300
=================================================
    145400 bytes,  13 chunks: "permanent memory          "
          pga heap          ds=0xf5441c0  dsprt=(nil)
     53132 bytes,   4 chunks: "free memory               "
          pga heap          ds=0xf5441c0  dsprt=(nil)
     32780 bytes,   1 chunk : "permanent memory          "
          top call heap     ds=0xf548380  dsprt=(nil)
     32200 bytes,   1 chunk : "permanent memory          "
          session heap      ds=0xb7a78ac0 dsprt=0xf5484a0
     31672 bytes,   1 chunk : "free memory               "
          top call heap     ds=0xf548380  dsprt=(nil)
     30036 bytes,   1 chunk : "Fixed Uga                 "
          pga heap          ds=0xf5441c0  dsprt=(nil)
```

Now see how to obtain process trace dumps with Oradebug.

Using Oradebug for Taking Processsstate Dump with Oracle 11g

In the event of a need to trace specific processes with Oracle 11g, a processstate dump can be taken with the following Oradebug command:

```
Oradebug dump processstate <level>
```

By default, the trace file will be output to the *user_dump_dest* directory set in the Oracle initialization or spfile for Oracle 11g and 10g.
Also, in addition to using the Oradebug tool, using an operating system tool such as truss for Solaris is beneficial as part of the process tracing activity.

To trace the processes, the following example using the trace for processstate dump is shown.

```
[oracle@raclinux1 trace]$ sqlplus "/as sysdba"

SQL*Plus: Release 11.1.0.6.0 - Production on Sat Aug 16 01:02:16 2008
```

```
Copyright (c) 1982, 2007, Oracle.  All rights reserved.

Connected to:
Oracle Database 11g Enterprise Edition Release 11.1.0.6.0 - Production
With the Partitioning, OLAP, Data Mining and Real Application Testing
options

SQL> Oradebug setmypid

Statement processed.

SQL> Oradebug unlimit

Statement processed.

SQL> rem process state dump with Oradebug
SQL> Oradebug dump processstate 10

Statement processed.

SQL> Oradebug tracefile_name
/u01/app/oracle/diag/rdbms/ora11g/ORA11G/trace/ORA11G_ora_28478.trc
SQL> exit
Disconnected from Oracle Database 11g Enterprise Edition Release 11.1.0.6.0
- Production
With the Partitioning, OLAP, Data Mining and Real Application Testing
options
[oracle@raclinux1 trace]$
[oracle@raclinux1 trace]$ view ORA11G_ora_28478.trc

*** 2008-08-16 01:03:26.456
Processing Oradebug command 'dump processstate 10'
====================================================

PROCESS STATE
-------------
Process global information:
     process: 0x37a56af0, call: (nil), xact: (nil), curses: (nil), usrses:
0x370476b0
     ----------------------------------------
  SO: 0x37a56af0, type: 2, owner: (nil), flag: INIT/-/-/0x00 if: 0x3 c: 0x3
   proc=0x37a56af0, name=process, file=ksu.h LINE:10286, pg=0
  (process) Oracle pid:18, ser:45, calls cur/top: (nil)/0x370b8dec
            flags: (0x0) -
            int error: 0, call error: 0, sess error: 0, txn error 0
  (post info) last post received: 0 0 0
            last post received-location: No post
            last process to post me: none
            last post sent: 0 0 0
            last post sent-location: No post
            last process posted by me: none
    (latch info) wait_event=0 bits=0
    Process Group: DEFAULT, pseudo proc: 0x37ab0390
```

Next is an explanation of how to use Oradebug to trace memory leak issues such as the ORA-04030 "Out of Process Memory" conditions with Oracle 11g.

Using Oradebug for Debugging Memory Issues for Oracle 11g

Often, memory leaks in Oracle 11g and previous releases are revealed with symptoms such as ORA-0600 and ORA-04030 errors generated to the Oracle trace files and *alert.log* file. To debug the issue with Oradebug, use a heapdump trace for the processes that are potential candidates for the root cause of these memory leaks. To do so, issue the following command:

```
Oradebug dump heapdump <level>
```

Here is an example of how to debug these memory issues for processes for Oracle 11g on Linux:

```
[oracle@raclinux1 trace]$ sqlplus "/as sysdba"

SQL*Plus: Release 11.1.0.6.0 - Production on Sat Aug 16 01:16:54 2008

Copyright (c) 1982, 2007, Oracle.  All rights reserved.

Connected to:
Oracle Database 11g Enterprise Edition Release 11.1.0.6.0 - Production
With the Partitioning, OLAP, Data Mining and Real Application Testing
options

SQL> Oradebug setmypid

Statement processed.

SQL> Oradebug unlimit

Statement processed.

SQL> -- take a heap dump for process memory issues such as ORA-04030
SQL> Oradebug dump heapdump 5

Statement processed.

SQL> Oradebug tracefile_name
/u01/app/oracle/diag/rdbms/ora11g/ORA11G/trace/ORA11G_ora_30421.trc

SQL> exit
```

```
Disconnected from Oracle Database 11g Enterprise Edition Release 11.1.0.6.0
- Production
With the Partitioning, OLAP, Data Mining and Real Application Testing
options

[oracle@raclinux1 trace]$ view ORA11G_ora_30421.trc

*** 2008-08-16 01:17:45.767
Processing Oradebug command 'dump heapdump 5'
********************************************************
HEAP DUMP heap name="session heap"  desc=0xb7de8ac0
 extent sz=0xffb8 alt=32767 het=32767 rec=0 flg=2 opc=2
 parent=0xf5484a0 owner=0x370476b0 nex=(nil) xsz=0xffb8 heap=(nil)
 fl2=0x60, nex=(nil)
EXTENT 0 addr=0xb7e00048
  Chunk b7e00050 sz=     28580     free        "                "
  Chunk b7e06ff4 sz=      8204     freeable    "kxsFrame4kPage "
  Chunk b7e09000 sz=      3912     free        "                "
  Chunk b7e09f48 sz=       172     freeable    "kgsc ht segs    "
  Chunk b7e09ff4 sz=      8204     freeable    "kxsFrame4kPage "
  Chunk b7e0c000 sz=      4084     free        "                "
  Chunk b7e0cff4 sz=     12300     freeable    "kxsFrame4kPage "
EXTENT 1 addr=0xb7df0058
  Chunk b7df0060 sz=     28744     perm        "perm           "   alo=28240
  Chunk b7df70a8 sz=      2072     free        "                "
  Chunk b7df78c0 sz=       492     freeable    "kxsc: kkspsc0  "
  Chunk b7df7aac sz=       172     freeable    "kgsc ht segs    "
  Chunk b7df7b58 sz=       492     freeable    "kxsc: kkspsc0  "
  Chunk b7df7d44 sz=       172     freeable    "kgsc ht segs    "
  Chunk b7df7df0 sz=       492     freeable    "kxsc: kkspsc0  "
```

Another useful function for process tracing for Oracle is possible with the Oradebug *procstat* command. Below is an example.

```
SQL> Oradebug setmypid

Statement processed.

SQL> Oradebug unlimit

Statement processed.

SQL> Oradebug procstat

Statement processed.

SQL> Oradebug tracefile_name
/u01/app/oracle/diag/rdbms/ora11g/ORA11G/trace/ORA11G_ora_31429.trc

[oracle@raclinux1 trace]$ view ORA11G_ora_31429.trc

*** 2008-08-16 01:24:29.624
Processing Oradebug command 'procstat'

----- Dump of Process Statistics -----
User time used = 1
System time used = 3
```

```
Maximum resident set size = 0
Integral shared text size = 0
Integral unshared data size = 0
Integral unshared stack size = 0
Page reclaims = 3900
Page faults = 0
Swaps = 0
Block input operations = 0
Block output operations = 0
Socket messages sent = 0
Socket messages received = 0
Signals received = 0
Voluntary context switches = 3
Involuntary context switches = 12
```

The command *oradebug dump errorstack* <level> can also be used to obtain more details for process memory usage. The following example illustrates how to obtain a complete process error stack with Oradebug.

```
SQL> Oradebug setmypid

Statement processed.

SQL> Oradebug unlimit

Statement processed.

SQL> Oradebug dump errorstack 1

Statement processed.

SQL> Oradebug tracefile_name
/u01/app/oracle/diag/rdbms/ora11g/ORA11G/trace/ORA11G_ora_32035.trc
SQL> exit
Disconnected from Oracle Database 11g Enterprise Edition Release 11.1.0.6.0
- Production
With the Partitioning, OLAP, Data Mining and Real Application Testing
options

[oracle@raclinux1 trace]$ view ORA11G_ora_32035.trc

*** 2008-08-16 01:29:19.096
Processing Oradebug command 'dump errorstack 1'

*** 2008-08-16 01:29:19.097
----- Error Stack Dump -----
----- SQL Statement (None) -----
Current SQL information unavailable - no cursor.

----- Call Stack Trace -----
calling          call     entry        argument values in hex
location         type     point        (? means dubious value)
---------------- -------- ------------ -----------------------
skdstdst()+38    call     kgdsdst()    BFFFAB78 ? 2 ?
ksedst1()+88     call     skdstdst()   BFFFAB78 ? 0 ? 1 ? A589366 ?
                                       851DC3E ? A589366 ?
ksedst()+33      call     ksedst1()+8  0 ? B7FDD564 ? 2050033 ? 0 ?
                                       FF ? 2004 ?
```

```
dbkedDefDump()+1046   call    ksedst()          0 ? 0 ? 0 ? 0 ? 0 ? 0 ?
ksedmp()+47           call    dbkedDefDump()    1 ? 0 ?
ksdxfdmp()+1432       call    00000000          1 ? 0 ? 0 ? 0 ? FFFFFFFF ?
                                                0 ?
ksdxen_int()+4606     call    00000000          BFFFC7D8 ? 12 ? 3 ?
                                                BFFFBC10 ? BFFFBBC0 ?
```

Notice that since no SQL statements are being executed for the session traced, no SQL is shown in the Current SQL information header for the trace file. If one suspends the process and takes a dump with Oradebug, there is the benefit of viewing exactly what tasks are performed by the process in question.

Next in this chapter is how to resolve database hang conditions with Oradebug.

Using Oradebug for Database Hang Analysis with Oracle 11g

Probably one of the most painful conditions that a busy DBA must face are angry calls from users complaining about slow performance or hanging applications in a production database environment. Database Hang Analysis is where Oradebug really shines as a major performance and debugging tool for Oracle problem resolution. As an added benefit, Oradebug can be used for single instance non-RAC Oracle databases as well as complex multiple node clustered Oracle RAC environments.

The following command is used to perform hang analysis for a single instance Oracle 11g database:

```
Oradebug hanganalyze <level>
```

For a clustered Oracle RAC environment, the syntax for *hanganalyze* commands is:

```
Oradebug setmypid
Oradebug setinst all
Oradebug -g all hanganalyze <level>
```

The levels defined for *hanganalyze* with Oradebug are as follows:

- 10: Dumps all processes (*ign state*)

- 5: Level 4 + Dump all processes involving wait chain (*nleaf*)

- 4: Level 3 + Dump leaf nodes (blockers) in wait chains (*leaf, leaf_nw, ign_dump state*)

- 3: Level 2 + Dump only processes considered in hang condition (*in_hang state*)

- 1-2: Generates only *hanganalyze* output with no process dump

Now that the syntax and levels associated with using the *hanganalyze* function have been explained, an example is provided to show how to perform hang analysis for Oracle 11g.

```
SQL> Oradebug setmypid

Statement processed.

SQL> Oradebug unlimit

Statement processed.

SQL> Oradebug hanganalyze 3
Hang Analysis in
/u01/app/oracle/diag/rdbms/ora11g/ORA11G/trace/ORA11G_ora_10509.trc
SQL> exit

[oracle@raclinux1 trace]$ view ORA11G_ora_10509.trc

*** 2008-08-16 02:50:45.862
Processing Oradebug command 'hanganalyze 3'

*** 2008-08-16 02:50:45.917
====================================================================

HANG ANALYSIS:
  instances (db_name.oracle_sid): ora11g.ora11g
  Oradebug_node_dump_level: 3
  analysis initiated by Oradebug
====================================================================

Chains most likely to have caused the hang:
  <no chains found>

====================================================================
No chains found.
====================================================================
Extra information that will be dumped at higher levels:

State of ALL nodes
([nodenum]/cnode/sid/sess_srno/session/ospid/state/[adjlist]):
```

```
*** 2008-08-16 02:50:45.918
====================================================================
END OF HANG ANALYSIS
====================================================================

*** 2008-08-16 02:50:45.919
====================================================================
HANG ANALYSIS DUMPS:
  Oradebug_node_dump_level: 3
====================================================================

State of LOCAL nodes
([nodenum]/cnode/sid/sess_srno/session/ospid/state/[adjlist]):

No processes qualify for dumping.

====================================================================
HANG ANALYSIS DUMPS: END
====================================================================
```

How to Suspend and Resume Processes with Oradebug

There are times when a slow running job process needs to be stopped and resumed at a later time so that a more critical batch job can run to completion. For example, if a nightly backup job is running longer than expected into the next day and needs to be stopped and resumed in Oracle, use Oradebug to perform this handy task. To illustrate, a walk-through example on how this works is provided.

First, find the shadow process that will be suspended with Oradebug.

```
SQL> select s.username, s.sid, p.spid
  2  from
  3  v$session s, v$process p
  4  where s.paddr=p.addr
  5  and
  6  s.username<>'SYS';

USERNAME                                   SID SPID
------------------------------- ---------- -------------------------
SH                                         140 18335
```

Now the Oradebug *suspend* command can be used to stop execution of the process in use by the SH user.

```
SQL> Oradebug setospid 18335
```

```
Oracle pid: 26, Unix process pid: 18335, image:
oracle@raclinux1.us.oracle.com (TNS V1-V3)
SQL> Oradebug suspend

Statement processed.
```

Then verify that the process has been suspended by a query against the
v$session_wait performance view:

```
SQL> select sid, event, state, wait_class
  2  from v$session_wait
  3  where sid=140;

      SID EVENT
--------- -----------------------------------------------------------------
STATE
------------------
WAIT_CLASS
-----------------------------------------------------------------
      140 SQL*Net message from client
WAITING
Idle
```

Now that the session is in waiting pattern, resume the process with the
Oradebug *resume* command as shown in the following example.

```
SQL> Oradebug resume

Statement processed.
```

Tuning SQL with Oradebug

Next to be covered is how to use Oradebug to trace parallel SQL
statements from a user session as well as learn how to trace parallel SQL
processes.

Recall earlier that two methods exist to set up a trace session with
Oradebug: one comes from a currently logged-in session using the
Oradebug *setmypid* command and the other finds the SID, SPID, and
PID for a currently running user process and then uses the Oradebug
setospid <SPID> command.

In addition to tracing and tuning SQL statements, there are several levels
for the 10046 SQL trace event listed below:

- 1: Enables tracing for SQL statements (default level)

- 4: Trace at level 1 + bind variable tracing

- 8: Trace at level 1 + wait event statistics

- 12: Trace at level 1 + bind variables and wait events

Level 12 is the highest trace level for SQL statement tracing and Level 1 is the default level for tracing SQL using the 10046 event.

Using Oradebug to Trace SQL for User Session

The first step to obtaining a SQL trace for a specific user session with Oradebug is to get the session information from the *v$session* performance view. This can be a little tricky as multiple sessions can be connected at the same time for a single user and schema. Therefore, the DBA needs a way to find the exact SPID matching the user session that will be traced.

To begin with, find the PADDR (procedure address) from *v$session* for the user session query:

```
SQL> select username, sid, serial#, paddr
  2  from
  3  v$session
  4  where username='SH';

USERNAME                             SID     SERIAL# PADDR
------------------------------ ---------- ---------- --------
SH                                   127         573 37A56AF0
```

Now that the SID, SERIAL#s, and PADDR for our user are located, find the SPID for the user before the trace for the user session's SQL statements can be enabled.

To obtain the SPID for the user session, simply plug in the details obtained from the previous query against the *v$session* view:

```
SELECT addr, pid, spid
FROM V$PROCESS
WHERE addr='<PADDR from V$SESSION>';
```

The following query against the *v$process* performance view will provide the details.

```
SQL> select addr, pid, spid
  2  from v$process
  3  where addr='37A56AF0';

ADDR            PID SPID
--------  ---------- -----------------------
37A56AF0         18 14298
```

So now that the SPID for the SH schema user session logged into Oracle is shown, set a new SQL trace for that session with Oradebug. The following exercise will show how to trace the SQL for this user session for Oracle 11g.

```
SQL> Oradebug setospid 14298
Oracle pid: 18, Unix process pid: 14298, image:
oracle@raclinux1.us.oracle.com (TNS V1-V3)
SQL> Oradebug unlimit

Statement processed.

SQL> Oradebug event 10046 trace name context forever, level 4

Statement processed.

SQL> Oradebug event 10046 trace name context off

Statement processed.
```

Once the SQL trace for the session has been completed, to disable and turn off the SQL trace, issue the following command:

```
Oradebug event 10046 trace name context off
```

Then examine the trace file generated from the session SQL trace:

```
*********************************************
----- Current SQL Statement for this session (sql_id=2bjk37s0qrdva)
update products
set prod_min_price=6
*********************************************
Starting SQL statement dump

user_id=85 user_name=SH module=SQL*Plus action=
sql_id=2bjk37s0qrdva plan_hash_value=-1831839393 problem_type=0
----- Current SQL Statement for this session (sql_id=2bjk37s0qrdva)
```

```
update products
set prod_min_price=6
sql_text_length=37
sql=update products
set prod_min_price=6
----- Explain Plan Dump -----
----- Plan Table -----

============
Plan Table
============
-------------------------------------+---------------------------------------+
| Id | Operation            | Name     | Rows | Bytes | Cost | Time     |
-------------------------------------+---------------------------------------+
| 0  | UPDATE STATEMENT     |          |      |       | 3    |          |
| 1  |  UPDATE              | PRODUCTS |      |       |      |          |
| 2  |   TABLE ACCESS FULL  | PRODUCTS | 72   | 2520  | 3    | 00:00:01 |
-------------------------------------+---------------------------------------+
Predicate Information:

====================== END SQL Statement Dump ======================
```

Since the raw trace file is difficult to read for SQL tracing, the DBA would benefit from using TKPROF to format the trace file into a more readable format.

```
[oracle@raclinux1 trace]$ tkprof ORA11G_ora_14298.trc
trace_sh_session_sql.rpt waits=yes aggregate=yes sys=no explain=sh/sh

TKPROF: Release 11.1.0.6.0 - Production on Sat Aug 16 03:47:15 2008

Copyright (c) 1982, 2007, Oracle.  All rights reserved.

[oracle@raclinux1 trace]$ view trace_sh_session_sql.rpt

TKPROF: Release 11.1.0.6.0 - Production on Sat Aug 16 03:47:15 2008

Copyright (c) 1982, 2007, Oracle.  All rights reserved.

Trace file: ORA11G_ora_14298.trc
Sort options: default
********************************************************************
count    = number of times OCI procedure was executed
cpu      = cpu time in seconds executing
elapsed  = elapsed time in seconds executing
disk     = number of physical reads of buffers from disk
query    = number of buffers gotten for consistent read
current  = number of buffers gotten in current mode (usually for update)
rows     = number of rows processed by the fetch or execute call
********************************************************************


********************************************************************

update products
set prod_min_price=6

call      count      cpu    elapsed      disk      query    current      rows
-------  ------  -------- ----------- ---------- ---------- ----------- ----------
Parse        1      0.05       0.13         9        221           0          0
```

```
Execute      1     0.02     0.08       3         4        75        72
Fetch        0     0.00     0.00       0         0         0         0
------- ------  --------  ---------  --------  --------  --------  ---------
total        2     0.07     0.21      12       225        75        72
```

Misses in library cache during parse: 1
Optimizer mode: ALL_ROWS
Parsing user id: 85   (SH)

```
Rows       Row Source Operation
-------    --------------------------------------------------------
      0    UPDATE   PRODUCTS (cr=4 pr=3 pw=3 time=0 us)
     72    TABLE ACCESS FULL PRODUCTS (cr=4 pr=3 pw=3 time=18 us cost=3
           size=2520 card=72)
```

Tracing Parallel SQL Processes for Oracle 11g

Earlier, the way to use Oradebug to trace SQL statements for user sessions with Oracle 11g was made known. Now tracking parallel SQL processes is covered.

As a test case, set the *parallel_min_servers* Oracle 11g initialization parameter to a high value and trace the activity.

```
SQL> alter system set parallel_min_servers=2;

System altered.

SQL> show parameter parallel_min_servers

NAME                                   TYPE          VALUE
-----------------------------------    -----------   --------------------
parallel_min_servers                   integer       2

[oracle@raclinux1 trace]$ ps -ef|grep p00
oracle   20881     1  0 04:04 ?        00:00:00 ora_p000_ORA11G
oracle   20883     1  0 04:04 ?        00:00:00 ora_p001_ORA11G
oracle   21019 15689  0 04:05 pts/2    00:00:00 grep p00
[oracle@raclinux1 trace]$
```

Now there are two parallel server processes running as shown in the previous example. These parallel SQL processes can be traced with Oradebug.

```
SQL> Oradebug setmypid

Statement processed.

SQL> Oradebug unlimit

Statement processed.
```

```
SQL> Oradebug event 10046 trace name context forever, level 4

Statement processed.

SQL> Oradebug event 10046 trace name context off

Statement processed.

SQL> Oradebug tracefile_name
/u01/app/oracle/diag/rdbms/ora11g/ORA11G/trace/ORA11G_ora_20809.trc

[oracle@raclinux1 trace]$ view ORA11G_ora_20809.trc

*** 2008-08-16 04:07:18.922
Processing Oradebug command 'event 10046 trace name context forever, level
4'

** 2008-08-16 04:12:42.319
STAT #2 id=1 cnt=179116 pid=0 pos=1 obj=0 op='PARTITION RANGE ALL PARTITION:
1 28 (cr=12282 pr=351 pw=351 time=29197 us cost=501 size=26646447
card=918843)'
STAT #2 id=2 cnt=179116 pid=1 pos=1 obj=70404 op='TABLE ACCESS FULL SALES
PARTITION: 1 28 (cr=12282 pr=351 pw=351 time=10155 us cost=501 size=26646447
card=918843)'

*** 2008-08-16 04:12:42.309
Processing Oradebug command 'event 10046 trace name context off'
```

The survey of the Oradebug utility will be concluded with a brief overview of the options available with Oracle 11g.

Syntax and Options for Oradebug

To obtain a list of all the functions and general commands available, the Oradebug *help* command will display these in the window within SQL*Plus as shown below in Oracle 11g Release 1 (11.1) on Red Hat Enterprise Linux platform.

```
SQL> Oradebug help

HELP            [command]              Describe one or all commands
SETMYPID                              Debug current process
SETOSPID        <ospid>               Set OS pid of process to debug
SETORAPID       <orapid> ['force']    Set Oracle pid of process to debug
SETORAPNAME     <orapname>            Set Oracle process name to debug
SHORT_STACK                          Get abridged OS stack
CURRENT_SQL                          Get current SQL
DUMP            <dump_name> <lvl> [addr]  Invoke named dump
DUMPSGA         [bytes]               Dump fixed SGA
DUMPLIST                             Print a list of available dumps
EVENT           <text>                Set trace event in process
SESSION_EVENT   <text>                Set trace event in session
DUMPVAR                  <p|s|uga>  <name>  [level]    Print/dump  a  fixed  PGA/SGA/UGA  variableDUMPTYPE
<address> <type> <count>  Print/dump an address with type info
SETVAR          <p|s|uga> <name> <value>  Modify a fixed PGA/SGA/UGA variable
PEEK            <addr> <len> [level]  Print/Dump memory
```

```
POKE            <addr> <len> <value>     Modify memory
WAKEUP          <orapid>                 Wake up Oracle process
SUSPEND                                  Suspend execution
RESUME                                   Resume execution
FLUSH                                    Flush pending writes to trace file
CLOSE_TRACE                              Close trace file
TRACEFILE_NAME                           Get name of trace file
LKDEBUG                                  Invoke global enqueue service debugger
NSDBX                                    Invoke CGS name-service debugger
-G              <Inst-List | def | all>  Parallel Oradebug command prefix
-R              <Inst-List | def | all>  Parallel Oradebug prefix (return outputSETINST
<instance# .. | all>      Set instance list in double quotes
SGATOFILE       <SGA dump dir>           Dump SGA to file; dirname in double quotesDMPCOWSGA     <SGA
dump dir> Dump & map SGA as COW; dirname in double quotes
MAPCOWSGA       <SGA dump dir>           Map SGA as COW; dirname in double quotes
HANGANALYZE     [level] [syslevel]       Analyze system hang
FFBEGIN                                  Flash Freeze the Instance
FFDEREGISTER                             FF deregister instance from cluster
FFTERMINST                               Call exit and terminate instance
FFRESUMEINST                             Resume the flash frozen instance
FFSTATUS                                 Flash freeze status of instance
SKDSTTPCS       <ifname> <ofname>        Helps translate PCs to names
WATCH                <address> <len>  <self|exist|all|target>  Watch a region of memoryDELETE
<local|global|target> watchpoint <id>    Delete a watchpoint
SHOW            <local|global|target> watchpoints       Show watchpoints
DIRECT_ACCESS   <set/enable/disable command | select query> Fixed table access
CORE                                     Dump core without crashing process
IPC                                      Dump ipc information
UNLIMIT                                  Unlimit the size of the trace file
PROCSTAT                                 Dump process statistics
CALL            [-t count] <func> [arg1]...[argn]  Invoke function with argumentsSQL>
```

Due to the new features with Oracle 11g, the available options for Oradebug may vary between releases of Oracle.

Summary

In this chapter, the following points about the Oradebug utility have been covered:

- Purpose and functionality of the Oradebug utility

- Initial setup and configuration for Oradebug

- How to view trace files generated by Oradebug

- Using Oradebug to dump SGA and PGA memory for Oracle 11g

- Hang Analysis with Oradebug

- View Oracle RAC events with Oradebug

- Tuning SQL with Oradebug

Network Troubleshooting for Oracle 11g

The last chapter illustrated how to use the powerful Oradebug tool for tuning and database problem analysis. In this chapter, some common Oracle database networking problems will be explained and coverage of useful tips and tools for resolving these types of issues will be provided.

Common Oracle 11g Network Errors

The Oracle networking environment for Oracle 10g and 11g is based on a client-server networking paradigm. Most implementations use TCP/IP-based networks for the Oracle Net services between the host OS and the database networking facilities. As such, the common components in a typical Oracle database environment for network communications consist of the client network connection and the server network connections.

Oracle Net Services provides the network services in the form of a client host-based *tnsnames.ora* file with entries stored for hosts and databases to be accessed across the network to the database server. The database server uses the Oracle listener to receive and send communication back to the client requests for databases across the network. Most common issues lie in the OS configuration for network services or a misconfiguration of either the client Oracle network environment or the server network environment for Oracle.

Some of the most common errors with Oracle networking include the following:

- **ORA-12154:** TNS: could not resolve service name

- **TNS-12545:** connect failed because target host or object does not exist

- **ORA-12157**: TNS: internal network communication error

- **ORA-12560**: TNS: protocol adapter error

Before showing how to resolve these common networking issues with Oracle, this chapter will review some useful tools for troubleshooting Oracle Net Services.

PING

One of the first steps to troubleshoot Oracle networking problems is to use the OS utility called PING, which is available for most operating systems. PING tests host connectivity. If the PING request fails, then the host OS networking services must be checked for configuration errors. For instance, the IP address may not be present in the */etc/hosts* file or the IP address may not be set up correctly in the DNS entry for the server. To show the syntax for the *ping* command, simply type the command at an OS shell or command prompt.

```
[oracle@raclinux1 ~]$ ping

Usage: ping [-LRUbdfnqrvVaA] [-c count] [-i interval] [-w deadline]
            [-p pattern] [-s packetsize] [-t ttl] [-I interface or address]
            [-M mtu discovery hint] [-S sndbuf]
            [ -T timestamp option ] [ -Q tos ] [hop1 ...] destination
[oracle@raclinux1 ~]$
```

To test host connectivity using the PING utility, use the following example:

```
[oracle@raclinux1 ~]$ ping raclinux1

PING raclinux1.us.oracle.com (192.168.203.1) 56(84) bytes of data.
64 bytes from raclinux1.us.oracle.com (192.168.203.1): icmp_seq=0 ttl=64 time=0.573 ms
64 bytes from raclinux1.us.oracle.com (192.168.203.1): icmp_seq=1 ttl=64 time=0.069 ms
64 bytes from raclinux1.us.oracle.com (192.168.203.1): icmp_seq=2 ttl=64 time=0.054 ms
64 bytes from raclinux1.us.oracle.com (192.168.203.1): icmp_seq=3 ttl=64 time=0.064 ms
64 bytes from raclinux1.us.oracle.com (192.168.203.1): icmp_seq=4 ttl=64 time=0.064 ms
64 bytes from raclinux1.us.oracle.com (192.168.203.1): icmp_seq=5 ttl=64 time=0.050 ms

--- raclinux1.us.oracle.com ping statistics ---

6 packets transmitted, 6 received, 0% packet loss, time 5014ms
rtt min/avg/max/mdev = 0.050/0.145/0.573/0.191 ms, pipe 2
Figure 4.1: Using the PING utility with Oracle 11g
```

Now that the PING utility has been illustrated as the first step for troubleshooting Oracle network issues, a similar utility available with Oracle 11g for resolving Oracle network connectivity issues called TNSPING will be examined.

TNSPING

The TNSPING utility is useful for testing connectivity for the Oracle network environment. The syntax for TNSPING is as follows:

```
tnsping <net service name> count
```

The count parameter is optional. Example:

```
[oracle@raclinux1 ~]$ tnsping raclinux1 5

TNS Ping Utility for Linux: Version 10.2.0.1.0 - Production on 08-SEP-2008
23:31:12

Copyright (c) 1997, 2005, Oracle.  All rights reserved.

Used parameter files:

Used HOSTNAME adapter to resolve the alias

Attempting to contact
(DESCRIPTION=(CONNECT_DATA=(SERVICE_NAME=raclinux1.us.oracle.com))(ADDRESS=(
PROTOCOL=TCP)(HOST=192.168.203.11)(PORT=1521)))
OK (0 msec)
OK (0 msec)
OK (0 msec)
OK (0 msec)
OK (10 msec)
```

Another example of TNSPING for Oracle 11g without the *count* parameter is shown below.

```
[oracle@raclinux1 ~]$ tnsping raclinux1

TNS Ping Utility for Linux: Version 11.1.0.6.0 - Production on 08-SEP-2008
23:52:08

Copyright (c) 1997, 2007, Oracle.  All rights reserved.

Used parameter files:

Used HOSTNAME adapter to resolve the alias
```

```
Attempting to contact
(DESCRIPTION=(CONNECT_DATA=(SERVICE_NAME=))(ADDRESS=(PROTOCOL=TCP)(HOST=192.
168.203.1)(PORT=1521))(ADDRESS=(PROTOCOL=TCP)(HOST=192.168.203.1)(PORT=1521)
)(ADDRESS=(PROTOCOL=TCP)(HOST=192.168.203.1)(PORT=1521)))
OK (30 msec)
```

Now it is time to move on to the more in-depth coverage of the next tool for Oracle Network troubleshooting, the LSNRCTL utility for Oracle 10g and 11g.

The LSNRCTL Utility for Oracle 11g

Once connectivity issues for hosts have been established, the next process flow to resolve outstanding Oracle networking errors is to use the Oracle Net 8 listener utility called LSNRCTL (Listener Control). The LSNRCTL utility provides many functions to start, stop, restart and load Oracle Net 8 Services for Oracle 10g and 11g environments. For example, to check the status for the default Oracle 11g listener, execute the *lsnrctl status* command shown next:

```
[oracle@raclinux1 ~]$ lsnrctl status

lsnrctl for Linux: Version 11.1.0.6.0 - Production on 10-SEP-2008 22:20:30

Copyright (c) 1991, 2007, Oracle.  All rights reserved.

Connecting to (ADDRESS=(PROTOCOL=tcp)(HOST=)(PORT=1521))

STATUS of the LISTENER
------------------------
Alias                     LISTENER
Version                   TNSLSNR for Linux: Version 11.1.0.6.0 - Production
Start Date                08-SEP-2008 23:39:36
Uptime                    1 days 22 hr. 40 min. 54 sec
Trace Level               off
Security                  ON: Local OS Authentication
SNMP                      OFF
Listener Log File
/u01/app/oracle/diag/tnslsnr/raclinux1/listener/alert/log.xml
Listening Endpoints Summary...

(DESCRIPTION=(ADDRESS=(PROTOCOL=tcp)(HOST=raclinux1.us.oracle.com)(PORT=1521
)))
Services Summary...
Service "ORA11G" has 1 instance(s).
  Instance "ORA11G", status READY, has 1 handler(s) for this service...
Service "ora11gXDB" has 1 instance(s).
  Instance "ORA11G", status READY, has 1 handler(s) for this service...
Service "ora11g_XPT" has 1 instance(s).
  Instance "ORA11G", status READY, has 1 handler(s) for this service...
```

```
The command completed successfully
[oracle@raclinux1 ~]$
```

The *lsnrctl* command has many options and functions. To show the
common help menu, simply type lsnrctl to open the utility then help as
listed in the figure below.

```
[oracle@raclinux1 ~]$ lsnrctl

lsnrctl for Linux: Version 11.1.0.6.0 - Production on 10-SEP-2008 22:22:00

Copyright (c) 1991, 2007, Oracle.  All rights reserved.

Welcome to lsnrctl, type "help" for information.

lsnrctl> help

The following operations are available
An asterisk (*) denotes a modifier or extended command:

start              stop             status
services           version          reload
save_config        trace            spawn
change_password    quit             exit
set*               show*

lsn\rctl> help start

start [<listener_name>] : start listener

lsnrctl> help stop

stop [<listener_name>] : stop listener

LSNRCTL> help services

service [<listener_name>] : get the service information of the listener

LSNRCTL>
```

As shown in the previous examples, all of the *lsnrctl* commands can be
executed directly from a command shell window or from a directly
opened session within the LSNRCTL utility.

One common error that arises in many Oracle 11g environments for
network issues is that services often are not available or presently
configured for Oracle Net 8. This will cause errors and connections to
the Oracle 11g database will fail. To verify that service names are correct
and present, use the *lsnrctl services* command as shown below.

```
[oracle@raclinux1 ~]$ lsnrctl

lsnrctl for Linux: Version 11.1.0.6.0 - Production on 10-SEP-2008 22:29:15

Copyright (c) 1991, 2007, Oracle.  All rights reserved.

Welcome to lsnrctl, type "help" for information.

lsnrctl > services

Connecting to (ADDRESS=(PROTOCOL=tcp)(HOST=)(PORT=1521))
Services Summary...
Service "ORA11G" has 1 instance(s).
  Instance "ORA11G", status READY, has 1 handler(s) for this service...
    Handler(s):
      "DEDICATED" established:0 refused:0 state:ready
         LOCAL SERVER
Service "ora11gXDB" has 1 instance(s).
  Instance "ORA11G", status READY, has 1 handler(s) for this service...
    Handler(s):
      "D000" established:0 refused:0 current:0 max:1022 state:ready
         DISPATCHER <machine: raclinux1.us.oracle.com, pid: 4010>
         (ADDRESS=(PROTOCOL=tcp)(HOST=raclinux1.us.oracle.com)(PORT=32796))
Service "ora11g_XPT" has 1 instance(s).
  Instance "ORA11G", status READY, has 1 handler(s) for this service...
    Handler(s):
      "DEDICATED" established:0 refused:0 state:ready
         LOCAL SERVER
The
 command completed successfully
lsnrctl>
```

If the service name appears in the listing for LSNRCTL, then one should be able to connect to that Oracle 11g service. Here is an example of an Oracle 11g Network error that can be resolved by using the correct service name.

```
[oracle@raclinux1 shm]$ sqlplus scott/oracle@ORA1i

SQL*Plus: Release 11.1.0.6.0 - Production on Wed Sep 10 22:33:41 2008

Copyright (c) 1982, 2007, Oracle.  All rights reserved.

ERROR:
ORA-12154: TNS:could not resolve the connect identifier specified
```

In this example, since there is not a service name configured with the name of ORA1i, the connection will hang at first and then eventually time out with an ORA network error message. Now if this incorrect service name is replaced with the following correct service name, then

Scott should be able to connect to the Oracle 11g database as shown below.

```
SQL*Plus: Release 11.1.0.6.0 - Production on Wed Sep 10 22:38:06 2008

Copyright (c) 1982, 2007, Oracle.  All rights reserved.

SQL> connect scott/oracle@ORA11G

Connected.
```

The majority of network errors are due to missing or incorrect entries on either the client or server configuration files for the *tnsnames.ora* and *listener.ora* with Oracle 10g/11g environments.

Summary

In this chapter, the most common problems that occur with Oracle networking environments were explained. Useful information on tools provided by Oracle for problem resolution of network errors within the Oracle database environment was presented. Here are the following topics that were covered:

- PING utility for testing host connections
- TNSPING utility for Oracle network connectivity
- LSNRCTL utility for Oracle listener configuration
- Solutions to common Oracle network issues

In the next chapter, methods for troubleshooting SQL and PL/SQL issues will be revealed.

Debugging SQL and PL/SQL

The last chapter showed how to debug network errors in Oracle database environments. This chapter will focus on common issues with SQL and PL/SQL programs. Details will be provided on useful tools and tricks for quickly debugging errors in SQL and PL/SQL applications for Oracle 11g. The coverage will begin with debugging tools for PL/SQL and SQL such as the useful package called *dbms_debug* (Database Management System Debug).

DBMS_DEBUG

The *dbms_debug* package is an undocumented internal package available for Oracle 11g that provides comprehensive debugging support for troublesome PL/SQL applications. One word of caution about using this package is in order. It should only be used in test and non-production environments unless support is provided by Oracle internal support. To show the package body, it is possible to issue a describe on *dbms_debug* to show all functions and parameters possible for this debugging package.

```
SQL> desc dbms_debug

FUNCTION ABORT RETURNS BINARY_INTEGER
PROCEDURE ATTACH_SESSION

Argument Name                    Type                    In/Out Default?
-------------------------------- ----------------------- ------ --------
DEBUG_SESSION_ID                 VARCHAR2                IN
DIAGNOSTICS                      BINARY_INTEGER          IN     DEFAULT
FUNCTION CONTINUE RETURNS BINARY_INTEGER
Argument Name                    Type                    In/Out Default?
-------------------------------- ----------------------- ------ --------
RUN_INFO                         RECORD                  IN/OUT
   LINE#                         BINARY_INTEGER          IN/OUT
   TERMINATED                    BINARY_INTEGER          IN/OUT
   BREAKPOINT                    BINARY_INTEGER          IN/OUT
   STACKDEPTH                    BINARY_INTEGER          IN/OUT
   INTERPRETERDEPTH              BINARY_INTEGER          IN/OUT
```

```
       REASON                          BINARY_INTEGER               IN/OUT
       PROGRAM                         RECORD                       IN/OUT
          NAMESPACE                    BINARY_INTEGER               IN/OUT
          NAME                         VARCHAR2(30)                 IN/OUT
          OWNER                        VARCHAR2(30)                 IN/OUT
          DBLINK                       VARCHAR2(30)                 IN/OUT
          LINE#                        BINARY_INTEGER               IN/OUT
          LIBUNITTYPE                  BINARY_INTEGER               IN/OUT
          ENTRYPOINTNAME               VARCHAR2(512)                IN/OUT
       OER                             BINARY_INTEGER               IN/OUT
    BREAKFLAGS                         BINARY_INTEGER               IN
    INFO_REQUESTED                     BINARY_INTEGER               IN      DEFAULT
 PROCEDURE DEBUG_OFF
 PROCEDURE DEBUG_ON

    Argument Name                  Type                    In/Out Default?
    ------------------------------ ----------------------- ------ --------
    NO_CLIENT_SIDE_PLSQL_ENGINE    BOOLEAN                  IN     DEFAULT
    IMMEDIATE                      BOOLEAN                  IN     DEFAULT
 FUNCTION DELETE_BREAKPOINT RETURNS BINARY_INTEGER
    Argument Name                  Type                    In/Out Default?
    ------------------------------ ----------------------- ------ --------
    BREAKPOINT                     BINARY_INTEGER          IN
 FUNCTION DELETE_OER_BREAKPOINT RETURNS BINARY_INTEGER
    Argument Name                  Type                    In/Out Default?
    ------------------------------ ----------------------- ------ --------
    OER                            BINARY_INTEGER          IN
 PROCEDURE DETACH_SESSION
 FUNCTION DISABLE_BREAKPOINT RETURNS BINARY_INTEGER
    Argument Name                  Type                    In/Out Default?
    ------------------------------ ----------------------- ------ --------
    BREAKPOINT                     BINARY_INTEGER          IN
 FUNCTION ENABLE_BREAKPOINT RETURNS BINARY_INTEGER
    Argument Name                  Type                    In/Out Default?
    ------------------------------ ----------------------- ------ --------
    BREAKPOINT                     BINARY_INTEGER          IN
 PROCEDURE EXECUTE
    Argument Name                  Type                    In/Out Default?
    ------------------------------ ----------------------- ------ --------
    WHAT                           VARCHAR2                IN
    FRAME#                         BINARY_INTEGER          IN
    BIND_RESULTS                   BINARY_INTEGER          IN
    RESULTS                        DBMS_DEBUG_VC2COLL      IN/OUT
    ERRM                           VARCHAR2                IN/OUT
 PROCEDURE GET_ENCODED_PKGVARS_FOR_CLIENT
    Argument Name                  Type                    In/Out Default?
    ------------------------------ ----------------------- ------ --------
    HANDLE                         RECORD                  IN
       NAMESPACE                   BINARY_INTEGER          IN
       NAME                        VARCHAR2(30)            IN
       OWNER                       VARCHAR2(30)            IN
       DBLINK                      VARCHAR2(30)            IN
       LINE#                       BINARY_INTEGER          IN
       LIBUNITTYPE                 BINARY_INTEGER          IN
       ENTRYPOINTNAME              VARCHAR2(512)           IN
    FLAGS                          BINARY_INTEGER          IN
    PBRUN_VERSION                  BINARY_INTEGER          IN
    STATUS                         BINARY_INTEGER          IN/OUT
    TIDL_BUF                       VARCHAR2                IN/OUT
    TIDL_VERSION                   BINARY_INTEGER          OUT
 PROCEDURE GET_ENCODED_STACK_FOR_CLIENT
    Argument Name                  Type                    In/Out Default?
    ------------------------------ ----------------------- ------ --------
    START_FRAME                    BINARY_INTEGER          IN
    FRAME_COUNT                    BINARY_INTEGER          IN
    FLAGS                          BINARY_INTEGER          IN
    MAX_STRING_LENGTH              BINARY_INTEGER          IN
    MAX_INDEX_VALUES               BINARY_INTEGER          IN
    PBRUN_VERSION                  BINARY_INTEGER          IN
    TIDL_BUF                       VARCHAR2                IN/OUT
    TIDL_VERSION                   BINARY_INTEGER          OUT
 FUNCTION GET_INDEXES RETURNS BINARY_INTEGER
    Argument Name                  Type                    In/Out Default?
```

```
------------------------------  ----------------------  ------  --------
VARNAME                         VARCHAR2                IN
FRAME#                          BINARY_INTEGER          IN
HANDLE                          RECORD                  IN
  NAMESPACE                     BINARY_INTEGER          IN
  NAME                          VARCHAR2(30)            IN
  OWNER                         VARCHAR2(30)            IN
  DBLINK                        VARCHAR2(30)            IN
  LINE#                         BINARY_INTEGER          IN
  LIBUNITTYPE                   BINARY_INTEGER          IN
  ENTRYPOINTNAME                VARCHAR2(512)           IN
ENTRIES                         TABLE OF BINARY_INTEGER OUT
FUNCTION GET_LINE_MAP RETURNS BINARY_INTEGER
Argument Name                   Type                    In/Out Default?
------------------------------  ----------------------  ------  --------
PROGRAM                         RECORD                  IN
  NAMESPACE                     BINARY_INTEGER          IN
  NAME                          VARCHAR2(30)            IN
  OWNER                         VARCHAR2(30)            IN
  DBLINK                        VARCHAR2(30)            IN
  LINE#                         BINARY_INTEGER          IN
  LIBUNITTYPE                   BINARY_INTEGER          IN
  ENTRYPOINTNAME                VARCHAR2(512)           IN
MAXLINE                         BINARY_INTEGER          OUT
NUMBER_OF_ENTRY_POINTS          BINARY_INTEGER          OUT
LINEMAP                         RAW                     OUT
PROCEDURE GET_MORE_SOURCE
Argument Name                   Type                    In/Out Default?
------------------------------  ----------------------  ------  --------
BUFFER                          VARCHAR2                IN/OUT
BUFLEN                          BINARY_INTEGER          IN
PIECE#                          BINARY_INTEGER          IN
FUNCTION GET_RUNTIME_INFO RETURNS BINARY_INTEGER
Argument Name                   Type                    In/Out Default?
------------------------------  ----------------------  ------  --------
INFO_REQUESTED                  BINARY_INTEGER          IN
RUN_INFO                        RECORD                  OUT
  LINE#                         BINARY_INTEGER          OUT
  TERMINATED                    BINARY_INTEGER          OUT
  BREAKPOINT                    BINARY_INTEGER          OUT
  STACKDEPTH                    BINARY_INTEGER          OUT
  INTERPRETERDEPTH              BINARY_INTEGER          OUT
  REASON                        BINARY_INTEGER          OUT
  PROGRAM                       RECORD                  OUT
    NAMESPACE                   BINARY_INTEGER          OUT
    NAME                        VARCHAR2(30)            OUT
    OWNER                       VARCHAR2(30)            OUT
    DBLINK                      VARCHAR2(30)            OUT
    LINE#                       BINARY_INTEGER          OUT
    LIBUNITTYPE                 BINARY_INTEGER          OUT
    ENTRYPOINTNAME              VARCHAR2(512)           OUT
  OER                           BINARY_INTEGER          OUT
FUNCTION GET_TIMEOUT_BEHAVIOUR RETURNS BINARY_INTEGER
FUNCTION GET_VALUE RETURNS BINARY_INTEGER
Argument Name                   Type                    In/Out Default?
------------------------------  ----------------------  ------  --------
VARIABLE_NAME                   VARCHAR2                IN
FRAME#                          BINARY_INTEGER          IN
SCALAR_VALUE                    VARCHAR2                OUT
FORMAT                          VARCHAR2                IN      DEFAULT
FUNCTION GET_VALUE RETURNS BINARY_INTEGER
Argument Name                   Type                    In/Out Default?
------------------------------  ----------------------  ------  --------
VARIABLE_NAME                   VARCHAR2                IN
HANDLE                          RECORD                  IN
  NAMESPACE                     BINARY_INTEGER          IN
  NAME                          VARCHAR2(30)            IN
  OWNER                         VARCHAR2(30)            IN
  DBLINK                        VARCHAR2(30)            IN
  LINE#                         BINARY_INTEGER          IN
  LIBUNITTYPE                   BINARY_INTEGER          IN
  ENTRYPOINTNAME                VARCHAR2(512)           IN
SCALAR_VALUE                    VARCHAR2                OUT
FORMAT                          VARCHAR2                IN      DEFAULT
FUNCTION INITIALIZE RETURNS VARCHAR2
Argument Name                   Type                    In/Out Default?
------------------------------  ----------------------  ------  --------
DEBUG_SESSION_ID                VARCHAR2                IN      DEFAULT
```

```
    DIAGNOSTICS                      BINARY_INTEGER           IN      DEFAULT
    DEBUG_ROLE                       VARCHAR2                 IN      DEFAULT
    DEBUG_ROLE_PWD                   VARCHAR2                 IN      DEFAULT
PROCEDURE PING
PROCEDURE PRINT_BACKTRACE
 Argument Name                      Type                     In/Out Default?
 ------------------------------     -----------------------  ------ --------
    LISTING                         VARCHAR2                 IN/OUT
PROCEDURE PRINT_BACKTRACE
 Argument Name                      Type                     In/Out Default?
 ------------------------------     -----------------------  ------ --------
    BACKTRACE                       TABLE OF RECORD          OUT
PROCEDURE PRINT_INSTANTIATIONS
 Argument Name                      Type                     In/Out Default?
 ------------------------------     -----------------------  ------ --------
    PKGS                            TABLE OF RECORD          IN/OUT
    FLAGS                           BINARY_INTEGER           IN
PROCEDURE PROBE_VERSION
 Argument Name                      Type                     In/Out Default?
 ------------------------------     -----------------------  ------ --------
    MAJOR                           BINARY_INTEGER           OUT
    MINOR                           BINARY_INTEGER           OUT
PROCEDURE SELF_CHECK
 Argument Name                      Type                     In/Out Default?
 ------------------------------     -----------------------  ------ --------
    TIMEOUT                         BINARY_INTEGER           IN      DEFAULT
FUNCTION SET_BREAKPOINT RETURNS BINARY_INTEGER
 Argument Name                      Type                     In/Out Default?
 ------------------------------     -----------------------  ------ --------
    PROGRAM                         RECORD                   IN
      NAMESPACE                     BINARY_INTEGER           IN
      NAME                          VARCHAR2(30)             IN
      OWNER                         VARCHAR2(30)             IN
      DBLINK                        VARCHAR2(30)             IN
      LINE#                         BINARY_INTEGER           IN
      LIBUNITTYPE                   BINARY_INTEGER           IN
      ENTRYPOINTNAME                VARCHAR2(512)            IN
    LINE#                           BINARY_INTEGER           IN
    BREAKPOINT#                     BINARY_INTEGER           OUT
    FUZZY                           BINARY_INTEGER           IN      DEFAULT
    ITERATIONS                      BINARY_INTEGER           IN      DEFAULT
PROCEDURE SET_DIAGNOSTIC_LEVEL
 Argument Name                      Type                     In/Out Default?
 ------------------------------     -----------------------  ------ --------
    DLEVEL                          BINARY_INTEGER           IN
FUNCTION SET_OER_BREAKPOINT RETURNS BINARY_INTEGER
 Argument Name                      Type                     In/Out Default?
 ------------------------------     -----------------------  ------ --------
    OER                             BINARY_INTEGER           IN
FUNCTION SET_TIMEOUT RETURNS BINARY_INTEGER
 Argument Name                      Type                     In/Out Default?
 ------------------------------     -----------------------  ------ --------
    TIMEOUT                         BINARY_INTEGER           IN
PROCEDURE SET_TIMEOUT_BEHAVIOUR
 Argument Name                      Type                     In/Out Default?
 ------------------------------     -----------------------  ------ --------
    BEHAVIOUR                       BINARY_INTEGER           IN
FUNCTION SET_VALUE RETURNS BINARY_INTEGER
 Argument Name                      Type                     In/Out Default?
 ------------------------------     -----------------------  ------ --------
    FRAME#                          BINARY_INTEGER           IN
    ASSIGNMENT_STATEMENT            VARCHAR2                 IN
FUNCTION SET_VALUE RETURNS BINARY_INTEGER
 Argument Name                      Type                     In/Out Default?
 ------------------------------     -----------------------  ------ --------
    HANDLE                          RECORD                   IN
      NAMESPACE                     BINARY_INTEGER           IN
      NAME                          VARCHAR2(30)             IN
      OWNER                         VARCHAR2(30)             IN
      DBLINK                        VARCHAR2(30)             IN
      LINE#                         BINARY_INTEGER           IN
      LIBUNITTYPE                   BINARY_INTEGER           IN
      ENTRYPOINTNAME                VARCHAR2(512)            IN
    ASSIGNMENT_STATEMENT            VARCHAR2                 IN
PROCEDURE SHOW_BREAKPOINTS
 Argument Name                      Type                     In/Out Default?
 ------------------------------     -----------------------  ------ --------
    LISTING                         VARCHAR2                 IN/OUT
```

```
PROCEDURE SHOW_BREAKPOINTS
 Argument Name                   Type                    In/Out Default?
 ------------------------------  ----------------------- ------ --------
 LISTING                         TABLE OF RECORD         OUT
PROCEDURE SHOW_BREAKPOINTS
 Argument Name                   Type                    In/Out Default?
 ------------------------------  ----------------------- ------ --------
 CODE_BREAKPOINTS                TABLE OF RECORD         OUT
 OER_BREAKPOINTS                 TABLE OF BINARY_INTEGER OUT
PROCEDURE SHOW_FRAME_SOURCE
 Argument Name                   Type                    In/Out Default?
 ------------------------------  ----------------------- ------ --------
 FIRST_LINE                      BINARY_INTEGER          IN
 LAST_LINE                       BINARY_INTEGER          IN
 SOURCE                          TABLE OF VARCHAR2(90)   IN/OUT
 FRAME_NUM                       BINARY_INTEGER          IN
PROCEDURE SHOW_SOURCE
 Argument Name                   Type                    In/Out Default?
 ------------------------------  ----------------------- ------ --------
 FIRST_LINE                      BINARY_INTEGER          IN
 LAST_LINE                       BINARY_INTEGER          IN
 SOURCE                          TABLE OF VARCHAR2(90)   IN/OUT
PROCEDURE SHOW_SOURCE
 Argument Name                   Type                    In/Out Default?
 ------------------------------  ----------------------- ------ --------
 FIRST_LINE                      BINARY_INTEGER          IN
 LAST_LINE                       BINARY_INTEGER          IN
 WINDOW                          BINARY_INTEGER          IN
 PRINT_ARROW                     BINARY_INTEGER          IN
 BUFFER                          VARCHAR2                IN/OUT
 BUFLEN                          BINARY_INTEGER          IN
 PIECES                          BINARY_INTEGER          OUT
FUNCTION SYNCHRONIZE RETURNS BINARY_INTEGER
 Argument Name                   Type                    In/Out Default?
 ------------------------------  ----------------------- ------ --------
 RUN_INFO                        RECORD                  OUT
   LINE#                         BINARY_INTEGER          OUT
   TERMINATED                    BINARY_INTEGER          OUT
   BREAKPOINT                    BINARY_INTEGER          OUT
   STACKDEPTH                    BINARY_INTEGER          OUT
   INTERPRETERDEPTH              BINARY_INTEGER          OUT
   REASON                        BINARY_INTEGER          OUT
   PROGRAM                       RECORD                  OUT
     NAMESPACE                   BINARY_INTEGER          OUT
     NAME                        VARCHAR2(30)            OUT
     OWNER                       VARCHAR2(30)            OUT
     DBLINK                      VARCHAR2(30)            OUT
     LINE#                       BINARY_INTEGER          OUT
     LIBUNITTYPE                 BINARY_INTEGER          OUT
     ENTRYPOINTNAME              VARCHAR2(512)           OUT
   OER                           BINARY_INTEGER          OUT
 INFO_REQUESTED                  BINARY_INTEGER          IN     DEFAULT
FUNCTION TARGET_PROGRAM_RUNNING RETURNS BOOLEAN

SQL>
```

Next to be illustrated is an example of how to deploy the *dbms_debug* package to debug some PL/SQL code. Create the test table and procedure to work the example using the debug features.

```
SQL> create table employee as
  2  select * from scott.emp;

Table created.

SQL> create procedure test_procedure is
  2  begin
  3      update employee
  4      set sal=nvl(sal,0)*2.6
  5      where deptno=10;
```

```
6       dbms_output.put_line('Rows: '||
7           sql%rowcount);
8  end;
9  /
```

Procedure created.

Here is the syntax to debug the new PL/SQL procedure:

```
ALTER PROCEDURE [procedure_name] COMPILE DEBUG
```

Now use a worked example to debug the PL/SQL code above.

```
SQL> alter procedure test_procedure compile debug;
```

Procedure altered.

Then initialize the environment to use *dbms_debug* with the following initialize procedure for the package shown below.

```
SQL> -- we need to synchronize the environment to use DBMS_DEBUG
SQL> var a varchar2(50)
SQL> exec :a := DBMS_DEBUG.INITIALIZE()

PL/SQL procedure successfully completed.

SQL> print a

A
-------------------------------------------------------008601640001
```

Now that there is the return code from the initialization procedure output from *dbms_debug*, the next step is to debug the PL/SQL application code. To begin, attach the session ID obtained earlier from the *dbms_debug.initialize* output using the *attach_session* procedure for *dbms_debug*. Then set a new breakpoint to debug the PL/SQL code by using the *dbms_debug.set_breakpoint* procedure as shown in the example below:

```
SQL> set serveroutput on
SQL> exec DBMS_DEBUG.ATTACH_SESSION('008601640001');

PL/SQL procedure successfully completed.

SQL> -- now we need to setup a breakpoint for line 3
SQL> -- which must be executable statement
SQL> DECLARE
```

```
 2    information DBMS_DEBUG.PROGRAM_INFO;
 3    bin_num    binary_integer;
 4    ret_code   binary_integer;
 5  BEGIN
 6    information.namespace :=
 7      DBMS_DEBUG.namespace_pkgspec_or_toplevel;
 8  information.name := 'TEST_PROCEDURE';
 9  information.owner :='SYS';
10  information.dblink := null;
11  information.line# := 3;
12  ret_code := DBMS_DEBUG.SET_BREAKPOINT(information,3,bin_num);
13  if ret_code != DBMS_DEBUG.SUCCESS then
14    DBMS_OUTPUT.PUT_LINE( ' Failed to set the breakpoint');
15  end if;
16  end;
17  /

PL/SQL procedure successfully completed.

SQL>
```

Now execute the test PL/SQL procedure that was created earlier to step through the debugging session using *dbms_debug*.

```
SQL> exec test_procedure;

Rows: 3
PL/SQL procedure successfully completed.
```

Due to the complex and poorly documented nature of the *dbms_debug* utility, most developers use third party PL/SQL developer tools such as Quest's software Toad for setting breakpoints and stepping through code execution due to the ease and graphical interface.

So far, only the surface of how to tap into the power of *dbms_debug* has been covered. More details are available in the documentation within the *dbmspb.sql* script located under *$oracle_home/rdbms/admin* including a detailed review of the procedures and functions for *dbms_debug*. The debugging review for PL/SQL and SQL will conclude with a description of how to use *dbms_profiler*.

DBMS_PROFILER

Another useful debugging tool for Oracle 11g PL/SQL is the *dbms_profiler* package which has been available since the Oracle 8i database release. The *dbms_profiler* package allows the Oracle DBA or developer to trace execution time for PL/SQL. This allows the DBA to identify the specific code within Oracle 11g which is a performance bottleneck and requires further tuning and analysis. Once the profiler data has been collected from the *dbms_profiler* session, it can be stored for further review and analysis.

As such, baseline collection can be used to measure PL/SQL performance over time and this is useful to the serious Oracle performance analyst and developer to best optimize PL/SQL applications. Many third party tools for Oracle performance such as Quest's Toad provide a graphical interface to profile execution of PL/SQL applications. While Oracle does not have such a tool, the command line interface in SQL*Plus can be used to profile PL/SQL code with the *dbms_profiler* package as a cost effective alternative to expensive third party tools.

To use the *dbms_profiler* package, it must first be installed by running the *profload.sql* script located under the */rdbms/admin* directory for Oracle 11g. The example below shows installing the *dbms_profiler* package and creating a user for testing out the features of the *dbms_profiler* package.

```
SQL> @?/rdbms/admin/profload.sql

Package created.

Grant succeeded.

Synonym created.

Library created.

Package body created.

Testing for correct installation
SYS.DBMS_PROFILER successfully loaded.

PL/SQL procedure successfully completed.
```

Now set up a new user for testing *dbms_profiler* called myprofiler:

```
SQL> create user myprofiler identified by myprofiler
  2   default tablespace users quota unlimited on users;

User created.
```

```
SQL> grant connect to myprofiler;

Grant succeeded.

SQL> grant select on plsql_profiler_runnumber to public;

Grant succeeded.

SQL> grant select, insert, update, delete on plsql_profiler_data to public;

Grant succeeded.

SQL> grant select, insert, update, delete on plsql_profiler_units to public;

Grant succeeded.

SQL> grant select, insert, update, delete on plsql_profiler_runs to public;

Grant succeeded.

SQL> create public synonym plsql_profiler_runs for
  2  myprofiler.plsql_profiler_runs;

Synonym created.

SQL> create public synonym plsql_profiler_units for
  2  myprofiler.plsql_profiler_units;

Synonym created.

SQL> create public synonym plsql_profiler_data for
  2  myprofiler.plsql_profiler_data;

Synonym created.

SQL> create public synonym plsql_profiler_runnumber for
  2  myprofiler.plsql_profiler_runnumber;

Synonym created.

SQL> connect myprofiler/myprofiler

Connected.
```

Next, load the *dbms_profile* details for the myprofiler user with the *proftab.sql* script located under the */rdbms/admin* directory for Oracle 11g.

```
SQL> sho user
USER is "MYPROFILER"
SQL> @?/rdbms/admin/proftab.sql

Table dropped.

Table dropped.

Table dropped.
```

```
Sequence dropped.

Table created.

Comment created.

Table created.

Comment created.

Table created.

Comment created.

Sequence created.

SQL>
```

Next to be covered are the procedures and functions for *dbms_profiler* and this chapter will conclude with an example of how to call this package to tune PL/SQL code. *Dbms_profiler* contains many procedures and functions for the performance analysis and tracing of PL/SQL code. To view the package specifications, use a describe on the package.

```
SQL> desc dbms_profiler

FUNCTION FLUSH_DATA RETURNS BINARY_INTEGER
PROCEDURE FLUSH_DATA
PROCEDURE GET_VERSION

Argument Name                    Type                    In/Out Default?
-------------------------------- ----------------------- ------ --------
 MAJOR                           BINARY_INTEGER          OUT
 MINOR                           BINARY_INTEGER          OUT
FUNCTION INTERNAL_VERSION_CHECK RETURNS BINARY_INTEGER
FUNCTION PAUSE_PROFILER RETURNS BINARY_INTEGER
PROCEDURE PAUSE_PROFILER
FUNCTION RESUME_PROFILER RETURNS BINARY_INTEGER
PROCEDURE RESUME_PROFILER
PROCEDURE ROLLUP_RUN
Argument Name                    Type                    In/Out Default?
-------------------------------- ----------------------- ------ --------
 RUN_NUMBER                      NUMBER                  IN
PROCEDURE ROLLUP_UNIT
Argument Name                    Type                    In/Out Default?
-------------------------------- ----------------------- ------ --------
 RUN_NUMBER                      NUMBER                  IN
 UNIT                            NUMBER                  IN
FUNCTION START_PROFILER RETURNS BINARY_INTEGER
Argument Name                    Type                    In/Out Default?
-------------------------------- ----------------------- ------ --------
 RUN_COMMENT                     VARCHAR2                IN     DEFAULT
 RUN_COMMENT1                    VARCHAR2                IN     DEFAULT
 RUN_NUMBER                      BINARY_INTEGER          OUT
PROCEDURE START_PROFILER
Argument Name                    Type                    In/Out Default?
-------------------------------- ----------------------- ------ --------
 RUN_COMMENT                     VARCHAR2                IN     DEFAULT
 RUN_COMMENT1                    VARCHAR2                IN     DEFAULT
 RUN_NUMBER                      BINARY_INTEGER          OUT
FUNCTION START_PROFILER RETURNS BINARY_INTEGER
Argument Name                    Type                    In/Out Default?
```

```
------------------------------- ---------------------- ------ --------
RUN_COMMENT                     VARCHAR2               IN     DEFAULT
RUN_COMMENT1                    VARCHAR2               IN     DEFAULT
PROCEDURE START_PROFILER
 Argument Name                  Type                   In/Out Default?
------------------------------- ---------------------- ------ --------
RUN_COMMENT                     VARCHAR2               IN     DEFAULT
RUN_COMMENT1                    VARCHAR2               IN     DEFAULT
FUNCTION STOP_PROFILER RETURNS BINARY_INTEGER
PROCEDURE STOP_PROFILER
```

To start and end profiler sessions for PL/SQL code, use the *start_profiler*
and *stop_profiler* procedures of the *dbms_profiler* package. First, create the
sample PL/SQL code and then use *dbms_profiler* with this example.

```
SQL> CREATE OR REPLACE PROCEDURE test_load_proc (p_iterations IN NUMBER) AS
  2  l_insert NUMBER;
  3  BEGIN
  4    FOR a in 1 .. p_iterations LOOP
  5      SELECT l_insert + 1
  6      INTO   l_insert
  7      FROM dual;
  8  END LOOP;
  9  END;
 10  /

Procedure created.
```

Next, add the start and stop procedures for *dbms_profiler* in a PL/SQL
wrapper.

```
SQL> declare l_result binary_integer;

  2  begin
  3
l_result:=dbms_profiler.start_profiler(run_comment=>'test_load_proc:
'||SYSDATE);
  4    test_load_proc(p_iterations=>1);
  5    l_result:=dbms_profiler.stop_profiler;
  6  end;
  7  /
```

Now run out the test PL/SQL procedure and view details from
dbms_profiler shown in the following example.

```
SQL> exec test_load_proc(1);

PL/SQL procedure successfully completed.

SQL> set lines 200
SQL> set trimout on
SQL> col runid format 99999
SQL> col run_comment format a50
```

```
SQL> select runid, run_date, run_comment, run_total_time

  2  from plsql_profiler_runs
  3  order by runid;

RUNID RUN_DATE  RUN_COMMENT                                     RUN_TOTAL_TIME
------ --------- -------------------------------------------------- ----------
    1 14-SEP-08 Start profiler: 14-SEP-08                           0
```

Once the *dbms_profiler* session is completed, look at the code which ran slowly for the myprofiler schema. Then query the *plsql_profiler_units* and *all_source* to obtain the details as shown in the following examples.

```
SQL> select unit_owner, unit_number, unit_name, unit_type, total_time
  2  from plsql_profiler_units
  3  where unit_owner='PROFILER' and unit_type='PROCEDURE' and
unit_name='TEST_LOAD_PROC';

UNIT_OWNER      UNIT_NUMBER UNIT_NAME             UNIT_TYPE   TOTAL_TIME
--------------- ----------- --------------------- ----------- --------
PROFILER                  2 TEST_LOAD_PROC        PROCEDURE            0

9 rows selected.
```

It is now illustrated that the test PL/SQL code ran for zero seconds and to view the line details for the code, query the *all_source* view as shown in the next example.

```
SQL> select line||' : '||text
  2  from all_source
  3  where owner='PROFILER'
  4  and type='PROCEDURE'
  5  and name='TEST_LOAD_PROC';

LINE||':'||TEXT
------------------------------------------------------------------------1 :
procedure test_load_proc
2 : (p_iterations IN NUMBER) AS
3 : l_insert NUMBER;
4 : BEGIN
5 : FOR a in 1 .. p_iterations LOOP
6 :   SELECT l_insert + 1
7 :   INTO l_insert
8 :   FROM dual;
9 : END LOOP;
10 : END;

10 rows selected.
```

After the *dbms_profiler* session is completed, use the *dbms_trace* package to perform additional trace analysis on the PL/SQL code.

Summary

This chapter wraps up all that has been offered concerning the realm of Oracle troubleshooting and debugging. Details were presented on the following tools for debugging PL/SQL and SQL code:

- *dbms_debug*

- *dbms_profiler*

The final chapter will explain the internal BBED utility and give examples of its use.

Core Analysis with BBED for Oracle 11g

The last chapter provided a concise guide for many useful performance tuning tools for Oracle 11g and prior releases. In this chapter, the use of the undocumented internal BBED utility for Oracle will be covered.

What is BBED?

The BBED tool is the block browser and editor tool. It is an internal undocumented tool used by Oracle internal support engineers to provide last resort assistance for database down issues with Oracle 11g and other releases for Oracle. As such, BBED provides the following support functions:

- Block Corruption Repair
- Data Recovery for deleted or damaged databases
- Forensic analysis for Oracle database security professionals

BBED is really a last resort tool for Oracle when all else has failed and the Oracle DBA has no good backup in place to restore and recover the data. However, due to the complex nature of BBED functions, this tool must be used with extreme caution as it can cause data loss when used carelessly. As such, it is advisable to only use BBED under the watchful guidance of Oracle support. If the curious DBA wishes to play with BBED, it is recommended to test it on a sandbox non-production system to learn how the tool works. Also of note, due to security vulnerability with Oracle, BBED is popular with Oracle database security professionals and hackers as a tool for bypassing standard Oracle database security mechanisms.

Warning: use of BBED without opening an Oracle SR
and the assistance of Oracle support will invalidate
the Oracle support contract!

How to Use the BBED Utility with Oracle 11g

Some useful tips and tricks will be provided in this chapter on using
BBED for accessing data and making changes to Oracle 11g, then
conclude with an example of how to perform data recovery with BBED
when data loss has occurred and no good backup exists. It truly is an
almost magical tool. However, note that Oracle 11g no longer includes
the binaries for BBED, so the 10g binaries will need to be copied over
to the 11g directory.

Although BBED is not available for Oracle 11g, it can still be used after
copying the binaries for the 10g release of the tool. As discussed in the
introduction configuration section earlier in the chapter, there is a need
to link the Oracle 10g BBED binaries to the Oracle 11g home binary
directory.

Following are the steps needed to set up BBED for Oracle 11g on
Linux. Take note that to set up BBED on Windows platform for Oracle
11g, one does not have to perform the make and linking steps as these
are UNIX and Linux platform specific steps.

For Linux:

1. Copy BBED libraries for Oracle 10gR2 *$oracle_home/rdbms/lib* to
   Oracle 11g:

   - *$ cp $ora10gr2_home/rdbms/lib/ssbbded.o*

   - *$ora11g_home/u01/app/oracle/product/11.1.0/11g/rdbms/lib*

   - *cpora10g_home/rdbms/lib/sbbdpt.o to$ora11g_home/rdbms/lib*

2. Copy the BBED Message files (note - this may vary):

- *$cp $ora10gr2_home/rdbms/mesg/bbedus.msb*

- *$ora11g_home/rdbms/mesg*

- *$ cp $ora10gr2_home/rdbms/mesg/bbedus.msg*

- *$ora11g_home/rdbms/mesg*

- *$ cp $ora10g_home/rdbms/mesg/bbedar.msb*

- *$ora11g_home/rdbms/mesg*

3. Perform make for BBED binaries for 11g:

- *make-f $ora11g_home/rdbms/lib/ins_rdbms.mk   BBED =$oracle_home/bin/bbed*

- *$oracle_home/bin/bbed*

4. Login to BBED with default password:

- cd *$oracle_home/bin./bbed*

5. Enter the BBED password which is blocked by default.

Configuration Steps for Using BBED with Oracle 10g

The procedures for BBED setup are similar for Oracle 10g release except that binaries come shipped already for the utility with Oracle 10g so there is no need to copy additional files. The following step will need to be performed to set up the BBED utility for use.

As the Oracle OS user account, link the binaries for BBED to Oracle 10g library directory for binaries:

```
[oracle@raclinux1 lib]$ cd $ORACLE_HOME/rdbms/lib

[oracle@raclinux1 lib]$ make -f ins_rdbms.mk $ORACLE_HOME/rdbms/lib/bbed.

[oracle@raclinux1 lib]$ file bbed
bbed: ELF 32-bit LSB executable, Intel 80386, version 1 (SYSV), for
GNU/Linux 2.2.5, dynamically linked (uses shared libs), not stripped
[oracle@raclinux1 lib]$

[oracle@raclinux1 ~]$ ls -al $ORACLE_HOME/rdbms/lib/bbed
```

```
-rwxr-xr-x  1 oracle oinstall 540337 Jul  9 23:26
/u01/app/oracle/product/10.2.0/db_1/rdbms/lib/bbed
```

After the initial setup has been performed without errors, start BBED:

```
[oracle@raclinux1 lib]$ pwd
/u01/app/oracle/product/10.2.0/db_1/rdbms/lib
[oracle@raclinux1 lib]$ ./bbed
Password:

BBED: Release 2.0.0.0.0 - Limited Production on Tue Aug 19 02:23:20 2008

Copyright (c) 1982, 2005, Oracle.  All rights reserved.

************* !!! For Oracle Internal Use only !!! ***************

BBED>
```

After logging into BBED, use the *help* command from within the utility to obtain more details on syntax:

```
BBED> help

HELP [ <bbed command> | ALL ]
BBED> help verify
VERIFY [ DBA | FILE | FILENAME | BLOCK ]
```

To show the current details for BBED configuration, use the show all command:

```
BBED> show all
        FILE#        0
        BLOCK#       1
        OFFSET       0
        DBA          0x00000000 (0 0,1)
        FILENAME
        BIFILE       bifile.bbd
        LISTFILE
        BLOCKSIZE    8192
        MODE         Browse
        EDIT         Unrecoverable
        IBASE        Dec
        OBASE        Dec
        WIDTH        80
        COUNT        512
        LOGFILE      log.bbd
        SPOOL        No
```

Introduction to Using BBED

BBED is a command line tool that has two modes of operation: edit and browse modes. To avoid potential errors that may cause problems with the database environment, it is advisable for beginners to start using BBED in browse mode at first. The table in the figure below provides the current available options for use with BBED.

BBED Option	Purpose
MODE	Sets the mode (edit or browse) for BBED
BLOCKSIZE	Set blocksize for data files
SPOOL	Spool output to bbed.log file
SILENT	Suppress output and send to standard output
CMDFILE	Filename that contains list of BBED commands to run.
LISTFILE	Files listed to edit
BIFILE	Filename for the before-image file. The default is bfile.bbd
PARFILE	Parameter file with BBED options
LOGFILE	The BBED logfile name. The default filename is log.bbd

Table 6.1: *BBED Command Options*

Since BBED requires many of the above options to perform various recovery and browsing tasks, it is beneficial to first create a *parfile* for use with the tool. Below is an example of a *bbed parfile* that was created using the vi editor for Linux with Oracle 10gR2:

```
[oracle@raclinux1 lib]$ cat bbed.par

blocksize=8192
listfile=/u01/app/oracle/product/10.2.0/db_1/rdbms/lib
mode=edit
```

The example *parfile* for BBED sets the blocksize to 8k and uses the edit mode of BBED. Edit mode is the required mode for BBED when changing data blocks with Oracle. Next, create a *listfile* for BBED that will include the name of the file that will be edited as well as the file ID for the Oracle *datafile* and the file size given in bytes. To gather the file details for the datafiles, issue the following query for Oracle:

```
SQL> select file#||' '||name||' '||bytes from v$datafile;

FILE#||''||NAME||''||BYTES
------------------------------------------------------------------
[oracle@raclinux1 lib]$ cat test.log
1 /u01/app/oracle/oradata/test/system01.dbf 503316480
2 /u01/app/oracle/oradata/test/undotbs01.dbf 26214400
3 /u01/app/oracle/oradata/test/sysaux01.dbf 241172480
4 /u01/app/oracle/oradata/test/users01.dbf 5242880
5 /u01/app/oracle/oradata/test/example01.dbf 104857600

5 rows selected.
```

Now that the file details for the Oracle data files are located, it is now time to create the *listfile* for BBED. Using the DBA's favorite editor such as vi, create the *listfile* for BBED:

```
[oracle@raclinux1 lib]$ cat test.log

1 /u01/app/oracle/oradata/test/system01.dbf 503316480
2 /u01/app/oracle/oradata/test/undotbs01.dbf 26214400
3 /u01/app/oracle/oradata/test/sysaux01.dbf 241172480
4 /u01/app/oracle/oradata/test/users01.dbf 5242880
5 /u01/app/oracle/oradata/test/example01.dbf 104857600
```

Of special note: This author was unable to use BBED to work with ASM-based Oracle 10g/11g database files. It may be supported internally, but based on testing for BBED utility with ASM and RAC environments for Oracle 10g, there may be a compatibility issue for the BBED utility for ASM with Oracle. It may be intentional to resolve security vulnerability issues that BBED presents to non-ASM databases for Oracle. The given examples will use non-ASM instances with Oracle 10g for instructional purposes.

> ⚠ BBED is not certified to work with Oracle 10g ASM environments!

Based on the observation that Oracle 11g release does not contain the BBED libraries/binaries, it appears that Oracle either has a new internal tool or has ended further support for this undocumented utility.

Using BBED Commands for Oracle 10g/11g

Due to the complex nature of BBED commands, it is important to discuss the most often used options for the tool before critical tasks can be performed. Next to be reviewed are the most commonly used commands for BBED.

An explanation of the common options for using BBED is crucial before tasks can be performed with this undocumented tool.

Set mode

This command toggles the edit or browse mode for BBED.

```
BBED> set mode browse

        MODE            Browse

BBED> set mode edit

        MODE            Edit
```

It is recommended that beginners and even veteran DBAs start off using BBED in browse mode to avoid potential errors that can cause data loss to critical Oracle databases. Once the DBA is comfortable with using BBED, then issue the *set mode* to edit quickly. It is best to be cautious with BBED.

Set listfile

This command sets the *listfile* containing the options for BBED file identification that were discussed earlier. An example:

```
BBED> set listfile 'test.log'

        LISTFILE        test.log
```

Set blocksize

The *set blocksize* command is used to set the blocksize when editing blocks for Oracle with BBED. For the example of 8k blocksize with the 10g database for Oracle, the command is:

```
BBED> set blocksize 8192

        BLOCKSIZE       8192
```

Info

This command lists the files being browsed or edited with BBED:

```
BBED> info

File#  Name                                            Size(blks)
-----  ----                                            ----------
    1  /u01/app/oracle/oradata/test/system01.dbf           61440
    2  /u01/app/oracle/oradata/test/undotbs01.dbf           3200
    3  /u01/app/oracle/oradata/test/sysaux01.dbf           29440
    4  /u01/app/oracle/oradata/test/users01.dbf              640
    5  /u01/app/oracle/oradata/test/example01.dbf          12800
```

Set filename

The *set filename* command is one of the first things that needs to be configured for BBED before performing complex tasks. The *set filename* command tells BBED to set the datafile as current object for edit or browsing based on the edit mode set for BBED.

```
BBED> set filename '/u01/app/oracle/oradata/test/users01.dbf'

        FILENAME        /u01/app/oracle/oradata/test/users01.dbf
```

Set dba

The *set dba* command in BBED is used to move to the current data block using the Oracle DBA (Data Block Address) format. The syntax for the *set dba* command is to place *file_id* then the block number. For example, if one wishes to set the Oracle DBA to block 100 for *file_id* number 5 which would tell BBED to move to the example datafile for block number 100, issue the following command to BBED:

```
BBED> set dba 5,100

     DBA            0x01400064 (20971620 5,100)
```

BBED then replies with the hexadecimal location details for the set Oracle DBA.

Set file

The *set file* command instructs BBED to move to the current file specified. Recall that to obtain the file ID, the *v$datafile* was queried earlier. For instance, if the desire is to edit the UNDO tablespace data file, issue the command to BBED:

```
BBED> set file 2

     FILE#          2
```

Set block

The *set block* command tells BBED which block to use for the current edit or browse session. The block specified is that configured with the currently set filename or file for BBED. Either the absolute block may be set or an offset value can be given for the current block using + or − symbols. For example, to set block 22 for current file, issue the command:

```
BBED> set block 22

     BLOCK#         22
```

For a relative block value +30 which would bring one to the absolute block number 52, use the following:

```
BBED> set block +30

     BLOCK#         52
```

Show

The *show* command displays the current BBED settings for all options. For example, the current environment for BBED is illustrated with the following example:

```
BBED> show
        FILE#           2
        BLOCK#          52
        OFFSET          0
        DBA             0x00800034 (8388660 2,52)
        FILENAME        /u01/app/oracle/oradata/test/undotbs01.dbf
        BIFILE          bifile.bbd
        LISTFILE        test.log
        BLOCKSIZE       8192
        MODE            Browse
        EDIT            Unrecoverable
        IBASE           Dec
        OBASE           Dec
        WIDTH           80
        COUNT           512
        LOGFILE         log.bbd
        SPOOL           No
```

It is shown that BBED is currently in browse mode using the *test.log listfile* with default blocksize set to 8k and with current filename set to the UNDO tablespace.

Show all

The *show all* command is similar to the previous *show* command for BBED but displays additional items. For example:

```
BBED> show all
        FILE#           2
        BLOCK#          52
        OFFSET          0
        DBA             0x00800034 (8388660 2,52)
        FILENAME        /u01/app/oracle/oradata/test/undotbs01.dbf
        BIFILE          bifile.bbd
        LISTFILE        test.log
        BLOCKSIZE       8192
        MODE            Browse
        EDIT            Unrecoverable
        IBASE           Dec
        OBASE           Dec
        WIDTH           80
```

```
        COUNT           512
        LOGFILE         log.bbd
        SPOOL           No
```

Set count

The *set count* command tells BBED how to set the number of bytes for the data block to be shown with the *dump* command. By default, BBED sets the block count to 512. However, in order to view an entire 8k block, the dump should be performed at intervals for a total of eight dumps at offsets for 0, 512, 1024, 1536, 2038, 2560, 3092, and 3604. If the count is set to a high value, more of the block contents will be dumped each time. For a smaller dump, set the count value to a smaller value.

Example:

```
BBED> set count 1024

        COUNT           1024
```

Map

This shows available mapping for the current block being edit/browsed. In addition, the *map* command can be used with the */v* option for verbose or more detailed output. This command outputs the offsets for the block including information for the data block header. For example:

```
BBED> map

 File: /u01/app/oracle/oradata/test/undotbs01.dbf (2)
 Block: 22                              Dba:0x00800016
 ------------------------------------------------------------
 Undo Data

 struct kcbh, 20 bytes                  @0

 struct ktubh, 132 bytes                @20

 ub1 freespace[380]                     @152

 ub1 undodata[7656]                     @532

 ub4 tailchk                            @8188
```

If the /v option for *map* command is used, more details are obtained:

```
BBED> map /v

 File: /u01/app/oracle/oradata/test/undotbs01.dbf (2)
 Block: 22                                  Dba:0x00800016
 ------------------------------------------------------------
 Undo Data

 struct kcbh, 20 bytes                      @0
    ub1 type_kcbh                           @0
    ub1 frmt_kcbh                           @1
    ub1 spare1_kcbh                         @2
    ub1 spare2_kcbh                         @3
    ub4 rdba_kcbh                           @4
    ub4 bas_kcbh                            @8
    ub2 wrp_kcbh                            @12
    ub1 seq_kcbh                            @14
    ub1 flg_kcbh                            @15
    ub2 chkval_kcbh                         @16
    ub2 spare3_kcbh                         @18

 struct ktubh, 132 bytes                    @20
    struct ktubhxid, 8 bytes                @20
    ub2 ktubhseq                            @28
    ub1 ktubhcnt                            @30
    ub1 ktubhirb                            @31
    ub1 ktubhicl                            @32
    ub1 ktubhflg                            @33
    ub2 ktubhidx[59]                        @34

 ub1 freespace[380]                         @152

 ub1 undodata[7656]                         @532

 ub4 tailchk                                @8188
```

Another added benefit to the *map* command for use with BBED is that if the *set* command has not already been given to set current block for edits, or if another block is to be examined while maintaining access to the currently set block, the BBED *map* command with the /v option allows these details to be accessed as shown in the following example.

Perhaps one wants to view the map for the first block of the example01 datafile with Oracle 10g using the *map* /v command:

```
BBED> map /v dba 5,1

 File: /u01/app/oracle/oradata/test/example01.dbf (5)
 Block: 1                                   Dba:0x01400001
 ------------------------------------------------------------
```

```
Data File Header

struct kcvfh, 676 bytes                        @0
    struct kcvfhbfh, 20 bytes                  @0
    struct kcvfhhdr, 76 bytes                  @20
    ub4 kcvfhrdb                               @96
    struct kcvfhcrs, 8 bytes                   @100
    ub4 kcvfhcrt                               @108
    ub4 kcvfhrlc                               @112
    struct kcvfhrls, 8 bytes                   @116
    ub4 kcvfhbti                               @124
    struct kcvfhbsc, 8 bytes                   @128
    ub2 kcvfhbth                               @136
    ub2 kcvfhsta                               @138
    struct kcvfhckp, 36 bytes                  @484
    ub4 kcvfhcpc                               @140
    ub4 kcvfhrts                               @144
    ub4 kcvfhccc                               @148
    struct kcvfhbcp, 36 bytes                  @152
    ub4 kcvfhbhz                               @312
    struct kcvfhxcd, 16 bytes                  @316
    word kcvfhtsn                              @332
    ub2 kcvfhtln                               @336
    text kcvfhtnm[30]                          @338
    ub4 kcvfhrfn                               @368
    struct kcvfhrfs, 8 bytes                   @372
    ub4 kcvfhrft                               @380
    struct kcvfhafs, 8 bytes                   @384
    ub4 kcvfhbbc                               @392
    ub4 kcvfhncb                               @396
    ub4 kcvfhmcb                               @400
    ub4 kcvfhlcb                               @404
    ub4 kcvfhbcs                               @408
    ub2 kcvfhofb                               @412
    ub2 kcvfhnfb                               @414
    ub4 kcvfhprc                               @416
    struct kcvfhprs, 8 bytes                   @420
    struct kcvfhprfs, 8 bytes                  @428
    ub4 kcvfhtrt                               @444

  ub4 tailchk                                  @8188
```

Set ibase

This command sets the internal number base. By default, BBED sets it
to decimal. It can be set to hexadecimal, octal or decimal. Using this
command allows the *set file*, *set offset*, and *set block* commands to use
another base instead of decimal. When the command is executed
successfully, BBED will return the current base value. For example, set
the *ibase* value to hexadecimal:

```
BBED> set ibase hex
```

```
          IBASE         Hex
BBED> set block +FF

          BLOCK#        307
```

Then switch to octal values:

```
BBED> set ibase octal

          IBASE         Oct
```

Next, set it back to decimal:

```
BBED> set ibase decimal

          IBASE         Dec
```

Dump

The *dump* command prints the contents of the block to the monitor screen. The *dump* command is used in conjunction with the *set count* command to display block data. For the syntax:

```
BBED> help d

DUMP[/v] [ DBA | FILENAME | FILE | BLOCK | OFFSET | COUNT ]
```

For example, to dump the contents for the USERS tablespace, issue the following *dump* command with BBED:

```
BBED> dump /v

 File: /u01/app/oracle/oradata/test/example01.dbf (5)
 Block: 16      Offsets:    0 to  255  Dba:0x01400010
 ------------------------------------------------------------
 06a20000 10004001 17cf0600 00000106 l .\uffff....@..\uffff......
 20cb0000 01002800 2bc80000 13cf0600 l  \uffff....(.+\uffff...\uffff..
 0000e81f 021f3200 09004001 04000600 l ..\uffff...2...@.....
 aa000000 3f008000 ab001a00 04200000 l \uffff...?....\uffff.... ..
 17cf0600 00000000 00000000 00000000 l .\uffff.............
 00000000 00000000 00000000 00000000 l ................
 00000000 00010400 ffff1a00 541f3a1f l ...........T.:.
 3a1f0000 04008b1f 7c1f711f 541f0000 l :.......|.q.T...
 00000000 00000000 00000000 00000000 l ................
 00000000 00000000 00000000 00000000 l ................
 00000000 00000000 00000000 00000000 l ................
 00000000 00000000 00000000 00000000 l ................
 00000000 00000000 00000000 00000000 l ................
 00000000 00000000 00000000 00000000 l ................
 00000000 00000000 00000000 00000000 l ................
```

```
00000000 00000000 00000000 00000000 1 ................
```
```
<16 bytes per line>
```

Examine Command for BBED

The *examine* command prints out raw data in text format for data blocks with BBED. It is useful for a forensic analysis tool when security breaches have occurred and the busy Oracle security professional needs to track down where data has been hacked or compromised in an Oracle database.

Using the help option, the syntax for the command can be viewed:

```
BBED> help x
EXAMINE[/Nuf] [ DBA | FILE | FILENAME | BLOCK | OFFSET | symbol | *symbol ]
</Nuf>:
```

```
N - a number which specifies a repeat count.
u - a letter which specifies a unit size:
  b - b1, ub1 (byte)
  h - b2, ub2 (half-word)
  w - b4, ub4(word)
  r - Oracle table/index row
f - a letter which specifies a display format:
  x - hexadecimal
  d - decimal
  u - unsigned decimal
  o - octal
  c - character (native)
  n - Oracle number
  t - Oracle date
  i - Oracle rowid
```

To use the *examine* command to view raw trace dump:

```
BBED> set dba 1,20

        DBA              0x00400014 (4194324 1,20)

BBED> x
kcbh.frmt_kcbh                              @1
--------------
 0xa2
```

How to Check for Block Corruption Using BBED for Oracle 10g/11g

One nice function in BBED is the *verify* command. This allows one to check for block integrity similar to the DBVERIFY utility. In fact, BBED calls the DBVERIFY utility when the *verify* command is issued from within the utility when checking for block corruption.

```
BBED> verify

DBVERIFY - Verification starting
FILE = /u01/app/oracle/oradata/test/example01.dbf
BLOCK = 16


DBVERIFY - Verification complete

Total Blocks Examined          : 1
Total Blocks Processed (Data)  : 1
Total Blocks Failing   (Data)  : 0
Total Blocks Processed (Index) : 0
Total Blocks Failing   (Index) : 0
Total Blocks Empty             : 0
Total Blocks Marked Corrupt    : 0
Total Blocks Influx            : 0

BBED>
```

Syntax for BBED

The complete syntax for the BBED utility is extensive. Since it is an undocumented tool, only Oracle internal engineers have the complete list of functions and syntax.

To obtain extended help items for BBED with Oracle 10g, use the following command:

```
BBED: Release 2.0.0.0.0 - Limited Production on Tue Aug 19 02:23:20 2008

Copyright (c) 1982, 2005, Oracle.  All rights reserved.

************* !!! For Oracle Internal Use only !!! ***************

BBED> help all

SET DBA [ dba | file#, block# ]
SET FILENAME 'filename'
```

```
SET FILE file#
SET BLOCK [+/-]block#
SET OFFSET [ [+/-]byte offset | symbol | *symbol ]
SET BLOCKSIZE bytes
SET LIST[FILE] 'filename'
SET WIDTH character_count
SET COUNT bytes_to_display
SET IBASE [ HEX | OCT | DEC ]
SET OBASE [ HEX | OCT | DEC ]
SET MODE  [ BROWSE | EDIT ]
SET SPOOL [ Y | N ]
SHOW [ <SET parameter> | ALL ]
INFO
MAP[/v] [ DBA | FILENAME | FILE | BLOCK ]
DUMP[/v] [ DBA | FILENAME | FILE | BLOCK | OFFSET | COUNT ]
PRINT[/x|d|u|o|c] [ DBA | FILE | FILENAME | BLOCK | OFFSET | symbol |
*symbol ]
EXAMINE[/Nuf] [ DBA | FILE | FILENAME | BLOCK | OFFSET | symbol | *symbol ]
</Nuf>:
N - a number which specifies a repeat count.
u - a letter which specifies a unit size:
  b - b1, ub1 (byte)
  h - b2, ub2 (half-word)
  w - b4, ub4(word)
  r - Oracle table/index row
f - a letter which specifies a display format:
  x - hexadecimal
  d - decimal
  u - unsigned decimal
  o - octal
  c - character (native)
  n - Oracle number
  t - Oracle date
  i - Oracle rowid
FIND[/x|d|u|o|c] numeric/character string [ TOP | CURR ]
COPY [ DBA | FILE | FILENAME | BLOCK ] TO [ DBA | FILE | FILENAME | BLOCK ]
MODIFY[/x|d|u|o|c] numeric/character string
       [ DBA | FILE | FILENAME | BLOCK | OFFSET | symbol | *symbol ]
ASSIGN[/x|d|u|o] <target spec>=<source spec>
<target spec> : [ DBA | FILE | FILENAME | BLOCK | OFFSET | symbol | *symbol
]
<source spec> : [ value | <target spec options> ]
SUM [ DBA | FILE | FILENAME | BLOCK ] [ APPLY ]
PUSH [ DBA | FILE | FILENAME | BLOCK | OFFSET ]
POP [ALL]
REVERT [ DBA | FILE | FILENAME | BLOCK ]
UNDO
HELP [ <bbed command> | ALL ]
VERIFY [ DBA | FILE | FILENAME | BLOCK ]
CORRUPT [ DBA | FILE | FILENAME | BLOCK ]

BBED>
```

The Find Command (f)

The *find* command allows the DBA to search for data within a block using BBED. It allows search on hex, numeric, or string data values within the data block for Oracle. Pattern searches can be from the top of the block, i.e. offset 0 by using the TOP parameter with the *find* command, or from the current block location using the current parameter. The /x option searches for hexadecimal values while the /c option searches for character data. In the following example, the search is for a hex value:

```
BBED> find /x FF TOP

 File: /u01/app/oracle/oradata/test/example01.dbf (5)
 Block: 16              Offsets:  104 to  359       Dba:0x01400010
 ------------------------------------------------------------------
 ffff1a00 541f3a1f 3a1f0000 04008b1f 7c1f711f 541f0000 00000000 00000000
 00000000 00000000 00000000 00000000 00000000 00000000 00000000 00000000
 00000000 00000000 00000000 00000000 00000000 00000000 00000000 00000000
 00000000 00000000 00000000 00000000 00000000 00000000 00000000 00000000
 00000000 00000000 00000000 00000000 00000000 00000000 00000000 00000000
 00000000 00000000 00000000 00000000 00000000 00000000 00000000 00000000
 00000000 00000000 00000000 00000000 00000000 00000000 00000000 00000000
 00000000 00000000 00000000 00000000 00000000 00000000 00000000 00000000
 00000000 00000000 00000000 00000000 00000000 00000000 00000000 00000000

 <32 bytes per line>
```

Summary

BBED is an advanced internal Oracle tool with no documentation available. A detailed analysis was provided on this undocumented internal tool for Oracle.

The review included the following points:

- Overview of BBED for Oracle

- Command options for BBED

- Using BBED to check for block corruption

- The commonly used syntax for BBED

Due to the incompatibility and/or lack of support for Oracle 11g and ASM environments, it is best to only use the BBED tool for releases prior to Oracle 11g that do not use ASM to manage Oracle files. Also, due to the internal nature of this tool, it is best to only use it for sandbox non-production Oracle environments. If the tool is used for production, it should ONLY be used with the guidance from Oracle support engineers.

It is the hope of the author that much has been learned from this guide. For comments and questions, feel free to visit the author's Oracle database tips and tricks blog online at http://oracle-magician.blogspot.com or send an email to mixxalot@yahoo.com.

Appendix:
References

Chapter 1: Introduction to Oracle 11g Debugging

11g Top New Features Summary
Metalink Note #466931.1

Using and Disabling the Automatic Diagnostic Repository (ADR) with
Oracle Net for 11g
Metalink Note #454927.1

11g: How To Package And Send ORA-00600/ORA-07445 Diagnostic
Information To Support
Metalink Note# 443529.1

Finding *alert.log* file in 11g
Metalink Note # 438148.1

11g: Understanding Automatic Diagnostic Repository
Metalink Note #422893.1

11g Diagnosability: Frequently Asked Questions
Metalink Note #453125.1

11g Install: Understanding about Oracle Base, Oracle Home and Oracle
Inventory locations
Metalink Note #454442.1

Oracle® Database Utilities
11g Release 1 (11.1)

Part Number B28319-02
http://tahiti.oracle.com/

Chapter 2: Performance Tuning Tools for Oracle 11g

Recommended Method for Obtaining 10046 trace for Tuning
Metalink Note # 376442.1

How to get a Trace for And Begin to Analyze a Performance Issue
Metalink Note #117129.1

QREF: TKPROF Usage- A Quick Reference
Metalink Note # 29012.1

TKPROF Simplistic Overview
Metalink Note # 41634.1

Overview Reference for SQL_TRACE, TKPROF and Explain Plan
Metalink Note # 199081.1

How to find the offending SQL from a trace file
Metalink Note # 154170.1

Using TKPROF to compare actual and predicted row counts
Metalink Note #214106.1

How to use the SQL Tuning Advisor
Mctalink Notc: # 262687.1
Automatic SQL Tuning- SQL Profiles
Metalink Note # 271196.1
What are the Default Parameters when Gathering Table Statistics
Metalink Note # 406475.1

Oracle Database Performance Tuning Guide
11g Release 1 (11.1)
B28274-01

http://tahiti.oracle.com/

Oracle® Database PL/SQL Packages and Types Reference
11g Release 1 (11.1)
Part Number B28419-03
http://tahiti.oracle.com/

Chapter 3: Using The Oradebug Utility for Oracle 11g

SUPTOOL: ORADEBUG 7.3+ (Server/Manager/SQL*Plus Debug
Commands)
Metalink Note # 29786.1

Database Hangs: What to collect for support
Metalink Note # 452358.1

How to Enable *sql_trace* for Another Session or in MTS Using Oradebug
Metalink Note # 1058210.6

Expert secrets on Oradebug, Ben Prusinski, May 2008
http://www.dba-oracle.com/t_oradebug_tips.htm

Diagnosing Database Hanging Issues
Metalink Note # 61552.1
Introduction to Oracle Diagnostic Events
Metalink Note # 218105.1
How to Use Oradebug to Get Trace File Name and Location
Metalink Note # 310830.1

How to find PID for setospid in Oradebug
Metalink Note # 105395.1

Taking Systemstate Dumps when You cannot Connect to Oracle
Metalink Note # 121779.1

How to List All the Named Events Set for a Database

Metalink Note #436036.1

Steps to generate *hanganalyze* trace files
Metalink Note # 175006.1

Database Tracefile is truncated at 2GB
Metalink Note # 208891.1

RAC Survival Kit: Troubleshooting a Hung Database
Metalink Note # 206567.1

Chapter 4: Network Troubleshooting for Oracle 11g

Log and Trace Facilities on NET v2
Metalink Note # 39774.1

10gR2 Dedicated Connections Intermittently Fail with TNS-12518
Metalink Note # 371983.1

Troubleshooting Guide TNS- 12518 TNS Listener could not hand off
client connections
Metalink Note # 550859.1
TNS-12542 Error When Executing Batch Jobs or in High Transaction
Environment
Metalink Note # 276812.1

Oracle Database Net Services Administrator's Guide
11g Release 1 (11.1), B28316-04, April 2008
http://tahiti.oracle.com/

Oracle Database Net Services Reference Guide
11g Release 1 (11.1), B28317-01, July 2007
http://tahiti.oracle.com/

Network debugging (TNS):

---

http://www.dba-oracle.com/t_troubleshooting_sql_net_connectivity_errors.htm

Chapter 5: Debugging SQL and PL/SQL

Oracle Database PL/SQL Language Reference
11g Release 1 (11.1), Part Number B29370-02
http://tahiti.oracle.com/

Oracle Database Advanced Application Developer's Guide
11g   Release   1   (11.1)   1   (11.1)
Part Number B28424-02
http://tahiti.oracle.com/

DBMS_DEBUG: Simple Example of Debugging An Anonymous Block
Metalink Note # 221346.1

SQL Debugging (TKPROF):
http://www.dba-oracle.com/tips_oracle_tkprof_utility.htm

Program debugging (10046):
http://www.dba-oracle.com/oracle_news/2004_7_9_rittman.htm

PL/SQL (*dbms_profiler*):
http://www.dba-oracle.com/oracle_news/2004_9_2_jenkins.htm

Implementing and Using the PL/SQL Profiler
Oracle Metalink Note: 243755.1

Oracle®   Database   PL/SQL   Packages   and   Types   Reference
11g   Release   1   (11.1)
Part Number B28419-03

Chapter 6: Core Analysis with BBED for Oracle 11g

How to Determine the Block Header Size

Metalink Note # 1061465.6

Unpublished Metalink
Note # 62015.1- SUPTOOL: BBED-7.3.2+ Database Block
Oracle Corp., March 2000

Disassembling the Oracle Data Block: A Guide to the BBED Browser
and Editor, Graham Thornton, 2005

OTN Forums, Oracle http://forums.oracle.com

Index

About the Author

Ben Prusinski

Ben Prusinski is an Oracle Certified Professional with 10 years of full-time experience as a database administrator and has written numerous articles and white papers on database management. Ben is also an active member of the San Diego and Orange County Oracle and IBM DB2 User Group community, and he has published various articles for customers and user groups on data management.

Ben has been working with databases including Oracle, Microsoft SQL Server, IBM DB2 UDB, Informix, MySQL, and PostgreSQL since 1996 and has accumulated over a decade of practical knowledge and experience with complex database migrations and support on how to best achieve results with large database migrations to the Oracle platform.

Ben enjoys training in martial arts and tai chi as well as travel to exotic locations in his free time outside of working on Oracle databases. He has traveled to over 15 countries in Latin America and Asia and has a passion for learning new foreign languages as well as cultural traditions.

www.ingramcontent.com/pod-product-compliance
Lightning Source LLC
Chambersburg PA
CBHW080427060326
40689CB00019B/4410